Luke for the Space Age Church

LUKE

for the Space Age Church

ELMER L. GRAY

BROADMAN PRESS • Nashville, Tennessee

ISBN: 0–8054–8111–7
4281–11

Library of Congress Catalog Card Number: 70–145981
Dewey Decimal Classification: 226.4
Printed in the United States of America
18.5 Jy 71 KSP

To

Martha, my wife

a good Sunday School teacher

Foreword

Church members in the space age need to look to Jesus and take new heart. Jesus, the ideal man and the Son of God, is both leader and example for Christians in these days of great scientific advance. He is their resource for personal strength and their secret power for spiritual conquest. He is the church's answer to the world's devastating charge of irrelevancy. Disciples of Jesus who dare to follow him personally in the decades ahead will have power to affect lives, will experience personal satisfaction and fulfilment, and will be the agents and implements of God's will. Where can churchmen gain the view of Jesus they need in order to follow him and act like him? Luke, the Gospel for every man of every age, can provide that view.

Today's men need a system of ultimates, a set of values, a religion that all men of all circumstances can find adequate. Christ can be to modern man both a personal example and a living authority. The Gospel of Luke was written to present him as the universal Lord. Therefore a fresh look at significant points in that Gospel would be timely. Let's look at Luke with this question in mind: What is there here that will help today's man know what he exists for and how he can accomplish that purpose?

Our first assumption is that the world has meaning and purpose. This concept is based on the conviction that God is eminent. He is in events that are happening around us. This means that life in general has purpose more than that of the moment. Meaning comes from divine intention. It determines happenings rather than being the results from them. We are born not just as a result of human biology but to accomplish the will of God. We are agents of freedom for good. We can believe this because of Jesus.

The approach in this study of the Gospel of Luke is devotional. The Scripture selections and comments may even be read as daily devotion thoughts over a period of a quarter. Jesus is presented as the example for today's church members. People of this age are influenced by the permissiveness of the sexual revolution, the materialism of both capitalism and communism, and the lawlessness of revolutionaries. The quality of the cultural climate is pragmatic and humanistic. It will help if we can see what Jesus did in a variety of circumstances to which we might relate. Therefore, incidents of the life of Jesus will be set forth as guides for us in meeting contemporary situations.

The twenty-four chapters of Luke have been divided into eleven units in order to make possible the development of themes. The themes of the units are meant to be helpful in stimulating thinking and also in suggesting practical application.

I have written the comments with several persons in mind. One has been a Sunday School teacher I know well. Also I have kept in mind a Sunday School class of men whom I taught for about three years at the Crievewood Baptist Church of Nashville, Tennessee.

I appreciate Golden Gate Baptist Theological Seminary's help in the production of this study.

My greatest hope is that it will be of help to Sunday School teachers and pupils and also to individuals in personal devotional studies.

ELMER L. GRAY

Dean
Golden Gate Baptist
Theological Seminary
Mill Valley, California

Contents

Luke for the Space Age Church

UNIT
1

Born to Be

Birth seems to demand a fulfilment. What are men born for? In these times the worth of an inividual life seems both to be affirmed and also to be denied more than in any other age. Lives have been spent to buy control of a hill in a battle area and the hill has been given up a few days later. The death of millions every year from causes that are preventable seems to say further that life is of little value. On the other hand, we go to extreme limits to preserve life for brief periods even when usefulness is gone. Concern for a lost child will send thousands into a wilderness area to spend days searching for him. What is a life worth? And what makes it valuable?

This question asked in the general or universal sense is rather academic. It may become more vital when a person questions the reason for his own existence. Who has not asked in some way, "For what was I born?"

What can be learned by birth and its significance from Luke's account of Christ? In the first two chapters of his Gospel, Luke tells of two births. These are the births of John the Baptist and of Jesus. In the report of these births we can see the importance both of heritage and also of environment. Furthermore, the working of God in one's total life from pre-birth and on is evident. The conclusion of the second chapter of Luke helps us to see life's Great Design. What if one could look at mankind as a whole, that is, at all races of all ages in one great panoramic view? He would see strife for survival, for security, for status, and for self-realization. The individual is caught up in this massive movement of humanity trying to assert its being.

Human beings are increasing upon this planet at a fantastic rate. The population increase of the world in three years is equal to the population of the United States. Is each birth important? Is the explosive increase of humanity acting like inflation in economy—decreasing the value of the individual? What are individuals born to be? And why does the human race exist?

Focus your attention on a baby. Over seventy million of them will be born this year. Think of a baby that you know. What are his potentials? A stranger might look at a baby and say, "He doesn't look now like he would ever amount to anything." On the other hand, doting grandparents could see in that infant great possibilities.

Let us look at the first two chapters of the Gospel of Luke to see the working of God in a life, the meaning of life, and life's purpose.

LUKE'S PREFACE

Luke 1:1–4

Why should there be more than just one report of the life of Jesus (1:1)? Luke and the other Gospel writers were not merely recording events. They wanted the facts that they reported to display the divine truth that they had accepted.

Luke had been a companion of Paul. He is mentioned three times in the New Testament. In Colossians, Paul referred to "Luke, the beloved physician." In 2 Timothy 4:11 Paul mentioned him with appreciation: "Only Luke is with me." Then in Philemon 24 Paul listed Luke as one of his "fellow labourers." As a fellow labourer of Paul, Luke spent some time in Caesarea where he had opportunity to talk with some of the earliest followers of Jesus and to gain information firsthand. Luke may have heard the story of Jesus' birth from Mary herself.

An old legend is that Luke was a painter. His writing was marked with both the preciseness of a doctor and the meaningfulness of an artist.

Luke was probably a Gentile, the only writer in the New Testament who was not a Jew. He wrote good Greek. He claimed he made extensive research in order to write his Gospel (1:2). He set the information in order so that it might have a meaningful effect upon the reader (1:3–4).

Luke identified his reader as "Theophilus." Some say that it is a general name that Luke intended to apply to any reader of his Gospel. The name means "Lover of God." In a sense, therefore, a person who loves God may look upon the Gospel of Luke as a direct message.

Let us pray that men may be characterized by good will and understand the message of angels, "Rejoice! The news is good."

BORN FOR A PURPOSE

Luke 1:5–25

John the Baptist was born to an old priest and his wife. His birth was supernatural in that both of his parents were well advanced in years. His father Zacharias had received a special revelation. He was promised a son (1:13). The birth of a person is an event of concern to God. Parents can turn to God to find help in understanding the birth of their children. A birth is a fresh indication of the presence of God and of the determination of God to do something more with the human race.

Just what can a baby born in these days amount to? In some circumstances he might die of hunger in his early years. In others, he might be molded into an instrument of death and destruction. In many situations, he may live as a part of his culture, preserving and transmitting human ways that have existed for generations. Or, he might participate in giant leaps in the advancement of mankind. What will make the difference? In the same desperate circumstances some infants have died from hunger and others have survived to become leaders. On the other hand persons with similar abilities have taken different courses, some to be filled with misery and to share it and others to become persons of good will. Is it proper to ask, what are you born to be? Is there something that your life must attain in order for it to be complete? What will it take for this to happen, for the possible to become reality? The angel told Zacharias that his son would be "great in the sight of the Lord" (1:15). It was said before his birth that he would turn people to the Lord and make ready a people prepared for the Lord (1:16–17).

Pray that we may be as effective in our day as John was in his.

A CHILD OF DESTINY

Luke 1:26–38

The birth of Jesus was unique. He was born to a young woman who was a virgin (v.27). She was a Jewish maiden of Galilee with a very common name, Mary, and she was engaged to a man by the name of Joseph. One of God's heavenly messengers, Gabriel, appeared to her with the news that God had chosen her to bear the Son of the Most High (v.32).

The child promised to Mary was destined to rule as David had but his kingdom would have no end. His work would relate to the past and continue forever. Every person born is linked to mankind's history. Whatever has been in man's long history is incarnated in those born today. Twentieth-century men may be future oriented but they stand on their high pinnacle as a result of the successful struggle of previous generations.

The promise made to Mary was incredible. She could not believe that which was logically impossible (v.34). People in this day of science must preserve the ability to accept truth that cannot be validated by the physical sense. The angel told Mary that the Holy Spirit would bring about the foretold event and that the child would be called "holy the Son of God" (v.35). In some ways God is in every birth but he was in the birth of Jesus in a special way. A prominent recent emphasis in theology was on the eminence of God. True, he is in the daily happenings of life, but we must also recognize that he will move in special ways to accomplish his purpose.

Mary responded, "Be it unto me according to thy word" (v.38). Asking for no sign, she joyfully accepted God's will.

Let us ask for God's will to be done now as it was in the birth of Jesus.

A MOTHER'S SONG

Luke 1:39–56

Mary had to talk to someone. How much could she believe what had happened to her? Would anyone else believe her? Whom could she trust? There was Elizabeth, old enough to be her mother, but also expecting a child. The angel had referred to Elizabeth and so the young unmarried maiden went to see her older cousin who, everyone said, was not able to have children. Here was someone who could understand and rejoice with her.

Elizabeth's response to Mary was reassuring. With more than human wisdom Elizabeth perceived the significance of Mary's experience. The older cousin, in a prophetic note and filled with the Holy Spirit, spoke of God's great blessing on Mary. Elizabeth referred to Mary's unborn child as her Lord and said that the child she carried in her womb had leaped with joy at Mary's greeting (v.44).

With that Mary was overjoyed and she sang. The first word of her song in an ancient Latin translation was "Magnificat" and this came to be the way people referred to her song.

The song of Mary is divided into two parts. Verses 46–49 express her rejoicing over God's blessing on her. Then verses 50–55 point to the meaning of the birth of her Son. Through him God would change things. He would overthrow and reject the proud, the mighty, and the rich. These are those who have misconceptions of their own importance, who pervert opportunities and positions into pedestals of power instead of means of ministry and who assign priority to gaining goods instead of benefiting brothers. Mary could see her son lifting high the humble and satisfying the hungry with good things. He would be at the side of God's people.

Let us commit ourselves to that which Mary foretold would be the concern of her Son.

WHAT'S IN A NAME?

Luke 1:57–80

A child born to parents late in life was a special blessing. In the male-oriented society a son was a double joy. Pride demanded that he be named after his father.

But—no! His mother, Elizabeth, old enough to be a grandmother, said, "He will be called John." Zacharias nodded and wrote, "His name is John" (v.63). That settled it. The father, dumb during the months of pregnancy, regained his speech and his first words were praise to God (v.64).

Why was a child's name so important? In New Testament times often a child was given a name with meaning. This child's name signified that he would not follow in his father's footsteps and that he was set apart from his family. His name indicated that he was a gift from God to accomplish a mission.

People were astounded at this happening and remembered it. They felt the child had an unusual future ahead of him. His name would keep reminding them of that.

Luke described Zacharias as filled with the Holy Spirit. This was a phrase he used both in his Gospel and in the book of Acts. When people are filled with the Holy Spirit, they can do things for God. Zacharias prophesied.

The prophecy of Zacharias is in two parts. Verses 68–75 tell of the redemption and deliverance that God would give his people through the Messiah. Verses 76–79 refer to the work of John as the Forerunner of the Messiah. He would come to be recognized as the prophet of the Most High God. He would prepare the way of the Lord. He would lead people to salvation and forgiveness of sins.

Pray that your life will be such that your name will remind people of your Lord.

HEAVEN'S BIRTH ANNOUNCEMENT

Luke 2:1–20

What if it were up to you to design and plan the setting for the birth of God's Son? Surely you would make it magnificent and awesome. However, this is not what we find in this well-known portion of the Christmas story.

Here is the report of the modest circumstances of the birth of the Son of God. He was born to a virgin after an eighty mile, arduous journey she had made with her new husband. On their arrival in the small town of Bethlehem they could find no room in the inn. This lack of room has become symbolic to the followers of Christ. They see in this event a foregleam of the rejection Jesus would experience.

Mary and Joseph camped with the animals. The baby was born and laid in the manger, the feed trough (v.7). No friends were present to rejoice with them. Nor were the customary musicians there to add joyful song to the occasion.

On a nearby hillside were shepherds with their flocks. These were simple men without substance from which to offer gifts to the Christ child. We can look on them as representative of earth's needy people. God's heavenly messenger, his angel, visited these men in the field (v.9). The experience was almost more than they could stand.

The angel announced that he brought good news of great joy for all people. He used three titles in referring to the new baby—Savior, Christ, Lord (v.11).

The angel was joined by a heavenly choir. Their song included praise to God and a promise of peace to men whom God favored (v.14).

The shepherds immediately wanted to see what God had brought to pass. They found Mary, Joseph, and the baby and reported their wonderful experience. Mary remembered these things and pondered their meaning.

Let the song of the angels be a model for your prayer today.

THE CHILD FOR ALL AGES

Luke 2:21–38

Identified by circumcision as a child of the covenant community, the son of Mary was given the name Jesus which meant "Jehovah is Salvation" (v.21).

Then Joseph and Mary took the infant Jesus to the Temple for a double ceremony. It was time for his redemption as the firstborn and for the sacrifice for Mary's purification. The sacrifice consisted of two young doves which poor people could offer in the place of a lamb.

They were met by an aged prophet named Simeon. Luke described him as being under the Holy Spirit. Simeon lived, assured he would see the Messiah (v.26). Holding the baby Jesus in his arms he spoke of his contentment. He could die now without regret. He had seen God's salvation. His life had been like waiting through the night for the sunrise.

Luke has been called the universal gospel. He reported that the angel's announcement was good news for all people. Then here in reporting Simeon's prayer he again referred to salvation prepared for all people.

Simeon spoke to Mary and he foretold what the significance would be of her son's life. Because of him many would fall and many would rise. Furthermore, he would be resisted by strong opposition. This would all be like a sword in the soul of Mary.

Another person of advanced years came in at that instant. This was Anna, an eighty-four year-old widow spending her remaining years in the Temple. Fasting and praying she served God night and day (v.37). When she saw the baby Jesus, she too recognized him as the Redeemer.

These two must have seemed to Luke to be representative of all devout, prayerful people.

Let us ask the Holy Spirit to guide us into a fuller understanding of the messiahship of Jesus.

HE KNEW WHO HE WAS

Luke 2:39–52

Was Jesus like other children? Luke reported he grew in four ways: physical, mental, social, and spiritual (vv.40, 52).

At twelve Jesus reached the age when a boy assumed the responsibilities of manhood. He became a bar mitzvah (son of the law). As an act of obedience to the law Jesus accompanied Joseph and Mary to Jerusalem to observe the Passover feast. After a week they started home. Mary with the women and Joseph with the men did not realize until the evening camp that they had left Jesus in Jerusalem (v.44).

With proper parental concern they returned to Jerusalem to seek him. In the Passover season the rabbis would assemble in the Temple area to teach and discuss the law openly, especially to the youth entering into manhood. There Mary and Joseph found Jesus. He was hearing and listening to the teachers. He was also asking questions (v.47). His action did not offend these learned men but it amazed them. They were astounded at the depth of his understanding.

Mary seemed displeased. She told Jesus that she and his father had been looking for him with anxiety (v.48).

Jesus corrected her reference. Many feel that Jesus knew fully at this time who he was. In response to Mary's reference to Joseph as his father, Jesus asked if it was not proper for him to be about the business, or in the house, of his Father (v.49). Here is the first recorded saying of Jesus.

With that then he obediently returned to Nazareth with them. What an example of responsible action!

Let us pray that we might have a sharp awareness of our relation to God and also practice service and ministry to our fellowmen.

UNIT
2

Options of Life

What will you make of life? Will you be like primitive man, a victim of environment, fearful of the unknown, and seeking primarily to survive? Will you spend your life accumulating substance in an effort to achieve security? Will you give yourself and what you have to help others and to win their approval and love? Will you join good causes and find a sense of personal worth and identification with mankind's progress? Will you strive for the greatest possible development of your full personality? Will you commit yourself wholly to the worship of God and ministry to those in need?

The demands and calls of life are evidenced in the preaching of John the Baptist. The divine imperative insists that men participate in the work of God. It is not surprising though that to such a lofty demand some respond so superficially. They would serve God if they could do it on their own terms. However, persons will have to decide what will take priority. If they make the work of the kingdom of God the priority, then some other things must be excluded. There are matters that cannot even be of fringe concern.

The call of God is not an invitation to engage in a vain endeavor. This may be seen in Jesus' baptismal experience. As he did that which was right, he was empowered by the Spirit and encouraged by the voice of God. One should choose to do the right. When he does, he may be assured of divine support.

The right is not always easy to know. Then, when a person knows what is right, he will not always find it easy to do. Life's options include both ends and means. Is it ever right to do a little wrong to accomplish something good? Can one justify wrong approaches and actions with the argument of right ends and purposes? The ultimate goal that one chooses must determine the nature of his immediate decisions.

The choices that one makes are experiences that may bring him into a fuller realization of his potential. A person should be concerned not only with increasing in knowledge but also with the development of spiritual power and skills. Certain personal abilities may be effective even in eternity. These are faith, hope, and love. In eternity it may be significant to what degree one can commit himself—that is Faith; or to what extent he can see the good—that is Hope; or to what extent he can accept others and give himself—that is Love. One needs to exercise the options that will result in growth in these skills. A person may grow spiritually as he follows the example of Jesus. That would mean to come to an awareness of his place in the kingdom of God and to make intentional use of his abilities to defeat evil and to help persons in need.

Life is real and its reality is more fully experienced as one wilfully commits himself to the work of God. Luke 3–4 are meaningful to us as we consider the options of life.

VOCATION AND SERVICE

Luke 3:1–14

The demands and the calls of life are exemplified by the preaching of John the Baptist.

John was like an Old Testament prophet. The word of God came to him in the wilderness (v.2). What does it mean to be called? One may be called to trust in Christ. He may also be called to a particular life service.

John was a prophet, proclaiming baptism as a mark of repentance and forgiveness (v.3). Because of his unique emphasis on baptism he came to be known as John the Baptist (or the Baptizer). His preaching and baptism had a purpose. In them he was preparing the way for one who would follow him. The gospel writers saw this as a fulfilment of Isaiah 40:3–5. The reference there is to the ancient custom of building a road for a king to travel on his journey. John was preparing the hearts of men for the coming of Christ.

John's message was not "good news" but rather the news of impending peril. He warned his hearers of judgment, of wrath to come (v.7). He questioned the motives of the multitudes who responded and compared them to poisonous snakes crawling out of a fire.

Repentance must not be superficial. It must result in fruit-bearing. Profession is not genuine if there is not corresponding practice. Racial or social relationship does not afford privilege or favor to the individual person (3:8).

John's ethical standards are apparent in 3:10–14. He called for men to share what they had with others who had nothing. He also called for men to be honest and considerate of others in their work situations. This is somewhat like Micah's call to men "to do justly, and to love mercy" (Mic. 6:8).

Life may be a response to God's call and a commitment to his service. By exercising this option you may help prepare hearts for Christ.

THEN JESUS CAME

Luke 3:15–22

Expectation was at a high (v.15). People were sure it was the time for the Messiah to come. They were even wondering in their hearts if John might be the Christ.

John assured them he was not the Messiah but that the Messiah was coming soon. He should not even be compared with the Messiah. John was baptizing with water. The One coming would provide a superior baptism. He would be so much greater than John that the Forerunner said he would not even be fit to be a slave to him. The baptism by the "coming one" would be with the Holy Spirit and with fire (v.16). Those who would come to him would experience the presence of God and his power. John further said that the Christ would separate the good from the bad like a harvester separating wheat from chaff. And, like chaff, the bad would be burned with an unquenchable fire (v.17). Nothing can stop God's judgment.

At this point Luke told about the end of the career of John. John both exhorted people and preached good news to them (v.18). He also reproved the ruler Herod Antipas for his corrupt, disgusting personal life. The act was courageous but it proved to be his undoing. He was arrested and imprisoned.

Then Jesus came to be baptized. Luke's description of the baptism of Jesus was quite brief. By his baptism Jesus took his stand with persons professing their repentance of sin; he forecast in action his death and resurrection; and he received the commendation of his Father in heaven.

The baptism of Jesus marked the beginning of his public ministry. Like an anointing the Holy Spirit came upon him in bodily form as a dove (v.22). Here was the evidence of God's approval and power.

Pray that we might act in the right way at the right time under the approval of God.

JESUS' FAMILY TREE

Luke 3:23–38

Here is a strange, unexpected insertion into Luke's report on Jesus.

The baptism of Jesus accompanied by the descent of the Holy Spirit on him marked the beginning of his public ministry. Luke then told Jesus' age and inserted here his genealogy. At this time Jesus was about thirty, perhaps a little over.

Why did Luke put the genealogical account in at this point in his gospel? Why didn't he place it with the birth record?

One's ancestry is not as important to many people today as it was in Bible times. However, when Luke designated his belief in Jesus as the Messiah, the Son of God, he knew that many would ask, "Is he a descendant of David?" Therefore at this point he traced his lineage, not only back to David and Abraham, but clear back to Adam. Luke affirmed that Jesus was the Son of David and also related to every man. Here is evidence of Luke's concern that Christ's redemption be seen as available to all mankind.

Luke's genealogy is different from Matthew's. Matthew ended his genealogy with Abraham and Luke with Adam (v.38). The two genealogies are different though in the lists from Joseph to David. Scholars have endeavored to explain this discrepancy by saying that one (Matthew) is a royal account and the other (Luke) is a priestly account or that one (Matthew) is Joseph's genealogy and the other (Luke) is Mary's. Other more fanciful explanations have been offered.

The value of the genealogy of Jesus is that it establishes the age-long intention of God to bring into the world the Messiah and that this Promised One would be identified by birth with both the chosen people and also with all mankind.

Rejoice over the fulfilment of the plan of God and give yourself anew to Jesus the Christ.

TEMPTATION

Luke 4:1–13

Don't be surprised if a high spiritual experience is followed by tension and temptation. This happened to Jesus. Following baptism, he was tempted. In this experience he confronted options in approaching his messianic work. They had to do with his very choice of life style. What kind of a Messiah would he be? Would he use his power to satisfy his needs? Would he seek worldly power at any price? Would he major on the winning of popular acclaim?

In the first temptation Jesus, hungry, looked at the stones in abundance and was tempted to turn them to bread (vv.2–3). His temptation was that of all mankind. Multitudes were starving. Should he not feed himself and them?   But there is more to life than eating. Jesus had come not to change rocks to bread but to change men into the children of God.

The second temptation was for Jesus to make secure his lordship over all by committing himself to any means whether they were in harmony with his goals or not. He was tempted to make a deal with the devil (vv.5–7). Others have been tempted to seek to accomplish good goals by using evil means. This amounts to a perversion of values, to the substitution of devil worship for the worship of God. Jesus affirmed that only God is worthy of a person's fullest devotion (v.8).

The third temptation, in Luke's order, was for Jesus to make a spectacular play for public acceptance (vv.9–10). Would it not be reasonable to demonstrate one's personal power to establish oneself and to influence others? Such was Jesus' temptation. Would not a crowd so influenced be justified in demanding increasingly novel displays? The end could become obscured in the means. Influence wrongly gained may not be rightly used.

Let us seek strength from God to resist temptation that would turn us aside from being what God wants us to be.

JESUS' INAUGURAL ADDRESS

Luke 4:14–30

Luke included at this point in his narrative an event recorded by other gospel writers later in their accounts. This incident is like an inaugural statement. Jesus positioned himself and revealed the approach he would take in his messianic work.

Jesus came to Nazareth his hometown. This incident seems to be a foregleam of what was to come. Here the role of the Christ was clarified; the superficial fascination of the curious was depicted and rejection by the proud was exposed.

In the synagogue Jesus was recognized as a well-known guest and invited to speak. According to the custom in synagogues Jesus stood to read the Scripture and sat down to speak (v.16). The passage he chose was a portion of Isaiah 61:1–2. It was important for people to realize that the ministry of Jesus was the fulfilment of the prophetic message. When he had read the Scripture and sat down, people looked at him with expectancy. His opening statement did not alarm them. They did not see its significance but nodded to each other as though he had favored them. Jesus seemed to be repelled by their attitude of false flattery. He had not come to entertain the curious. With abruptness he indicted his hearers for expecting favoritism from him. He would no more make a meaningless show of his power than Elijah and Elisha did in their day (vv.26–27). They had performed greater miracles for foreigners than they had for their own people. Thus Jesus implied that he had come to proclaim God is Lord of all and salvation is for all people rather than a favored race.

The blast of Jesus' rebuke inflamed his hearers. In murderous wrath they seized him and took him to a high precipice to throw him over to his death (v.29). But he passed through the crowd and left them.

Take courage and positionize yourself whatever the cost.

JESUS' USE OF POWER

Luke 4:31–44

How times change! In 1960 a reference to demons would have sounded old fashioned if not actually primitive. However in the seventies such a reference would be timely.

Jesus was an astonishing person. He spoke authoritatively without quoting another authority. He walked unafraid among people who lived in fear of the unknown. He faced a test when a well- known demon-possessed man in Capernaum challenged him in the synagogue. The man expressed fear of Jesus and acclaimed him to be the Holy One of God (v.34). Jesus interrupted the man and commanded silence. He did not seem to desire this kind of testimony. With a word he commanded the devil to leave the man. Everyone present was amazed and they asked each other how it could have happened (v.36). They had not heard any mysterious words or seen any magic signs. Jesus' authority was something new to them.

From the synagogue Jesus went to the home of Simon Peter. He found Simon's mother-in-law with a high fever. He came to her bedside and with a word of rebuke to the fever he healed her (v.39). An incidental lesson may be seen in the response of the mother-in-law. She got up and began to wait on others. Jesus gives health and strength for service.

Many were brought to Jesus then for healing. Jesus healed them but again refused to permit improper acclaim of his divinity.

Jesus sought time by himself but crowds were always hunting him. People begged him not to leave them but he told them he must share the good news with others. He said his mission was to preach the kingdom of God (v.44). He had used his power and authority to defeat evil and to help people.

What power and authority do you have? Is it committed to the defeat of evil and to the help of people?

Life Commitments

By commitment and loyalty a person shapes his life. Many people have not thought where they are headed in life. They have not wilfully made commitments of themselves to ideas, to causes, or to persons. A person may act with initiative and choose how his life will be spent and invested. How will a person spend his time? To what will he give his energy and ability? For what is he willing to die and to live?

Chapters 5, 6, and 7 of Luke may help us consider the commitment one can make of his life.

To respond to Jesus may mean, in instances, to accept the new and reject the old. It may mean that one will have to recognize that persons are more valuable than rules or procedures. Opposition will often develop at this point. One must be sure of his full commitment to Christ or he will be unable to face opposition he will meet. Commitment is tested, though, by opposition. Critics will not limit their scrutiny and charges simply to ideas. They will also examine a person's actions and life. Jesus is our example. He challenged his critics and demanded that they judge whether he had done good or evil, whether he had saved life or destroyed it. Good actions should reinforce good words.

Some things are worthy of life commitment. It is good to be able to discern true value and not to be distracted either by material gain or by popular acclaim. Jesus instructed people about the essence of true happiness and about the inadequacy of materialism.

Much of life depends upon interpersonal relations. One should, with thought, determine his disposition toward others beginning even with those who are his enemies. A person who can love his enemies will not have trouble with acquaintances and friends. A good guideline is to do the good to others that you would like to have done to you. That is the Golden Rule. But who can follow it? One can find help in being merciful by remembering God's mercy.

Another concern in life commitment is personal honesty and morality. This may seem rather old-fashioned and sentimental in this day. What would happen in this sophisticated era if Christians in great numbers began to speak out honestly for Christ and to live lives of personal purity? What effect would this have on our society? A society or a nation cannot survive the decay of its moral structure. Immediate attention and prompt action are needed to eliminate the cancer of immorality and to encourage personal purity and social righteousness.

Life needs to be fully committed to Christ. This will mean a solid foundation for a good building. It will be able to weather all storms. When the worst that can happen has blown over, that committed life will stand like a monument to Christ and guide to others in the various predicaments of life.

The commitment that one makes of his life determines the place that love will have in it. How much will he really care for others? Will he go out of his way to help them? The motivation that one has to help others will depend on his love for them. Likewise the love that one says he has is proved by his actions. One should not be afraid for his intentions to be judged by his actions. Along with this dedication of life to others a person is reinforced in his commitment when he understands the significance of his actions of ministry.

RESPONSE TO JESUS

Luke 5:1–16

Jesus went after people like a fisherman going after fish. There were people who could not be reached if he limited his preaching to congregations in synagogues. Therefore, he took to the open with his ministry. On an occasion a crowd sought him out on the beach of Lake Gennesaret (also called the Sea of Galilee). Jesus spoke to the crowd from a boat he had commandeered from Simon. The boat was available because of the commitment of its owner (v.3).

After addressing the crowd, Jesus led Simon in an experience that set him to the task of seeking to win people. He told Simon to go out to the deep and lower the nets for a catch. This instruction was given after a night of failure. Simon was tired and the circumstances seemed unfavorable. Yet he would do whatever Jesus said (v.5). What trust! Simon and his co-workers went out and came in with boats so loaded they were sinking. He fell at Jesus' knees and called himself a sinful man. Such a sense of conviction came from his realization of the divine power displayed by Jesus. Then Jesus called him to commit himself to people rather than to fish (v.10). Simon, James, and John heard him and leaving all they followed him. Their response is an example for Christians today. People are more important than things. Some of the greatest advances yet to be made are in the understanding of people.

Ministry to the needy is becoming a greater concern. Jesus is our example in this Christian action. A leper asked Jesus for help. Lepers were the human rejects of that day. Not even their loved ones would touch them. Life was humiliating, painful, and oh, so lonely. A man whom no one would touch looked to Jesus and Jesus touched him. Jesus said, "I will: be thou clean" (v.13).

Follow Christ; it will mean committing yourself to helping people. What do you see in life? Jesus saw people.

WHAT TO DO WITH SINS AND SINNERS

Luke 5:17–32

A person's sins can paralyze him. One time when Jesus was surrounded by Pharisees and legal scholars, he was healing people and a paralytic was brought to him (v.16). The paralyzed man had a greater problem than paralysis. He was hurting more from shame than from disease. He may have been like some who are so guilt-conscious that they cannot tolerate themselves and cannot believe that anyone else will tolerate them. But he had friends who had faith and who cared for him. Therefore they brought him to Jesus. Jesus saw that more was wrong with him than illness. His indisposition was more spiritual than physical. Jesus said to him, "Man, your sins are forgiven" (v.20). As much as this man needed forgiveness, there were those who would argue technically about forgiveness. Some would withhold forgiveness until the offender admitted the fullest degree of blame. Critics of Christ insisted that only God could forgive sins (v.21). They were right and they were wrong. Only God can forgive persons for perverting their beings. However, Jesus taught people to pray for forgiveness just as they forgave others. What is forgiveness? It is helping a person to understand that he is loved and accepted in spite of and in the face of his wrongdoing. A forgiven person can rise above any circumstances. Jesus demonstrated that his power to forgive and his power to heal were the same (v.24).

Levi was a tax collector. He was a sinner just as is every man, but the society around him seemed to be determined that his condemned state should not be changed. Jesus called him and he left all to follow him. The scribes and Pharisees murmured. They challenged Jesus for associating with sinners (v.30). He responded that he had come to associate with them because they needed him. He would heal them.

Can you forgive people and love them? You can if you will follow the example of Jesus.

36

OLD CUSTOMS AND NEW WAYS

Luke 5:33–39

Being a Christian is a life commitment that is exclusive. A person who becomes a Christian may have to give up some old habits and customs. This may seem to suggest that Christianity is oppressive and burdensome but the opposite is true. Christianity is liberative and enlightening. The action of Jesus upon the conversion of Levi aroused questions in the minds of the Pharisees and scribes. Jesus had been a guest at a feast given by Levi. His critics saw this as an opportunity to challenge him (v.33).

What should be the life attitude of Christians? Should they become committed mourners? Some people think that the only way you can be religious is to be long-faced. That seemed to be the view of Jesus' critics. He advised them that fasting is out of place at a wedding. Following Jesus is as joyous as a wedding celebration. Who could fast while Jesus was near! The time would come, said Jesus, when he would be gone and his followers would fast. The cross seemed to loom on the horizon.

People who live in changing times are not always aware of the new. Jesus' statement about the new can be applied to our day. He suggested that the new should not be just patched on to the old (v.36). He also said that the new could not be limited to old forms: it would destroy the old (v.37). He also recognized that a person who was used to the old might not like the taste of change (v.38). In Jesus' day, as in our day, the new was overwhelming the old. In days of change we can take courage from the words of Jesus. Christians should keep minds and hearts open continually to the new leadership of Christ.

Conversion is a change. In a way it is the beginning of a lifetime of change or growth. Let your change be in the direction of the mind of Christ.

POLICY VERSUS PERSONS

Luke 6:1–11

What is happening to Sunday? Should some things not be done on Sunday that may be all right on other days? Is the recognition of Sunday as a special day an ancient custom being continued into the present without reason?

In the time of Jesus the sabbath, which was the seventh day of the week instead of the first, was a day restricted by negative regulations. Tradition had made it oppressive, an instrument of dehumanization and depersonalization. The radical difference between Jesus' approach to religion and that of Judaism is clear in this Scripture passage. Rules and regulations should exist in order to help men individually and as groups, to find fulfilment of their lives.

These two incidents, reported by Luke, relate to the sabbath but the issue is much larger.

Does it seem fantastic that scholarly authorities would criticize Jesus and his disciples for plucking and eating some grain as they walked through a field on the sabbath (v.2)? Is this like some instances today where people forget the great works of evangelism and ministry to argue over procedures and tradition? Jesus' critics were not just arguing for argument's sake. They were defending their life commitment to the religion of law and works. They could see that what Jesus did was a threat to their way and position. Jesus responded by reminding them how in extreme need a favored person set aside a regulation (vv.3–4). Persons are more important than rules.

Luke reported another incident to give further light regarding law in general and sabbath observance in particular. The opponents of Jesus watched him to see if he would heal on the sabbath (v.7). Sure enough, Jesus healed the man, but before he did, he challenged his critics (v.9).

Let us meet our days and use our strength with purpose.

HAPPINESS OR MISERY

Luke 6:12–26

What will you get out of life? It will depend a lot on what you want and the price you are willing to pay.

After a night of prayer Jesus chose twelve men from the disciples (vv.12–13) to become the leaders of the Christian movement. They were not men of note. Jesus can do his work through ordinary men committed to him. From here on these men were with Jesus (v.17).

A crowd assembled as Jesus was healing people. This was an opportunity for him to instruct them regarding life's objectives and values. With a shock treatment approach Jesus startled his hearers with paradoxical statements. Poverty, starvation, and sorrow are surely the worst of human conditions. But Christians do not have to be overwhelmed by circumstances. Are there followers of Christ who are poor? They may be poor but they can be happy because the kingdom of God belongs to them (v.20). When a person, even though poor, is under God's direction, he is fortunate. When a person, even though hungry, is a follower of Christ, he is satisfied (v.21). Then even a weeping Christian can be happy because he knows his sorrow and frustration are only temporary. Furthermore, a person who suffers because of Christ can exalt in advance over the victory that he foresees by faith (vv.22–23). Blessed, indeed, are Jesus' disciples.

Jesus emphasized the importance of one's set of values. Those who magnify their possessions had better enjoy them because that is all they will ever get (v.24). Those who have plenty may be miserable because they have a hunger that food won't satisfy (v.24). Those who refuse to be serious will face a day they can't laugh through (v.25). And being well-spoken of can result in a life of loss and ruin (v.26).

Reexamine your set of values and change the price tags where needed.

THE GOLDEN RULE

Luke 6:27–38

Christians have a good defense. How are they on the offense? What do they do when they face enemies?

Jesus said the thing to do when you face enemies is to love them (v.27). Never does a Christian have a greater opportunity to demonstrate his commitment to Christ than when facing vicious opponents. Take the initiative. Find something good to do to those who hate you. Disarm the one cursing you by speaking to him with goodwill and pray for those who abuse you (v.28). To the violent person offer no resistance but seek to discover and meet his need (v.29). Help everyone who asks help (v.30). Many would say this is going too far. One should be more concerned about helping people than about being reasonable. He should realize what he wants others to do to him and then do that to them (v.31). This idea has been called "The Golden Rule." Perhaps we have set it on a pedestal to admire rather than place it in our hearts to practice.

Christians should be willing to love their enemies. They are no different from sinners if they love only those who love them (v.32). Does being a Christian make any real difference? Does the community in which he lives benefit from his grace and goodness? Does he help all kinds of people in need? Will he withhold help from persons of other views, religions, or social status? How can we who have been helped so much by God not be merciful and generous to all persons around us?

Here we are, though, human beings with the ability to discern good and evil, the proper and the improper. Is it not right for us to use this discernment and judge whether people are worthy of help? No. Let us give and help others without such judgments. We can use our judgment on ourselves. Let us treat others with mercy. You can't lose by measuring generously to others (v.38).

40

HONESTY OR HYPOCRISY

Luke 6:39–49

People need one another but whom can they trust? What if they seek help from someone who can't see any better than they can? If the way of life is not clear to you, be honest about it. Don't offer help you do not have to give. The ditch may be your destiny (v.39). It is hypocrisy to criticize others and to deny your own faults which may exceed those of others (v.41). If a person has the ability to judge, he should exercise it on himself. The best teacher is a skilled learner. The best adviser may be one who has corrected himself.

A person should be honest clear through his being. One's actions and words may be compared to the fruit of a tree. The fruit is consistent with the kind of a tree producing it. You can tell what kind of a tree it is by looking at the fruit it bears (v.44). And you can tell what a person is by the kind of things he says and does. If at the center of his being he is good, he will do what is good even under pressure. However, a bad person will do and say bad things (v.45). You can't deliver something good in words if all you have in storage in your heart is bad.

The worst hypocrisy of life is to call Christ one's Lord and then not to do what he says (v.46). The commitment one makes of himself to Christ determines the degree of his strength in life's storms. A full commitment to Christ is like building a house on a rock foundation. When tensions and trouble are at their worst that life will stand firm and unshaken (v.48). On the other hand, when a person does not commit himself to Christ in obedience to his call, his life, even though it may have a good appearance, is like a house without a foundation. Pressures damage it and increase to the point of ruining it (v.49).

Honesty is not easy. Our greatest need is to practice it with God, that is, to confess our sins and ask his forgiveness.

WHO CARES FOR OTHERS?

Luke 7:1–10

Wouldn't it be wonderful if people cared for one another? Instead they seem to find satisfaction in erecting barriers and in excluding others from their fellowship. Luke made the point over and over that the gospel was for all. Here he described the faith of a Gentile army officer.

Jesus came to Capernaum where a certain slave was ill and dying. He belonged to a centurion, an army officer. A dying slave was a liability and not an asset. It would not have surprised anyone for a centurion to throw a sick slave out to die. This centurion was different. He cared for his slave (v.2) and would do anything to help him.

Then he heard of Jesus. He may have felt hesitant, as a Gentile, to approach Jesus so he asked Jewish elders, whom he had befriended, to make intercession for him (v.3). The elders carried his petition to Jesus and assured him that the centurion was worthy of his favor (v.4).

Jesus started to go to the centurion's house. The officer had thought further on the situation. He realized that if Jesus could heal, it was with authority. This was a quality of life he understood. He himself obeyed authority and exercised it (v.8). Immediately he sent friends with a second message. He did not feel worthy of Jesus taking time for him. If Jesus would speak, the servant would be healed (v.7).

Luke recorded the reaction of Jesus. This seems to be the most important thing about the incident. Jesus said the greatest faith he had found up to that point was that of this man, a Gentile (v.9). This event shows that unlikely people can care for others and can believe in Jesus. There is hope for all of us.

By the way, in case you were wondering, they found the slave well when they got back to the house (v.10).

Surprise someone today with your concern and faith!

PROVE YOURSELF

Luke 7:11–23

Plan your life. Then commit yourself to the action necessary to fulfil your plan. Jesus indicated that he was willing for his actions to be accepted as proof of his messiahship.

As Jesus approached the little town of Nain, he met a funeral procession (v.12). The only son of a widow had died and friends and neighbors had joined her in the expression of sorrow. This is life, isn't it? Tragedy and sorrow are realities. Suffering is all around us. How should it be met? Should it be the concern only of those who are touched by it? Can one in trouble even hope for help from God? The action of Jesus encourages us. At this point in his gospel Luke referred to Jesus as Lord (v.13). The Lord had compassion and told the widow not to weep. Doesn't this prove something about God? Jesus spoke to the dead (v.14). The youth who was dead sat up and talked (v.15). When people saw what Jesus did, they respected him and concluded that he was a prophet from God (v.17). He had proved himself to them.

Luke turned his attention next to one who was less easily impressed than the crowd. Word of the actions of Jesus had come to John the Baptist in prison. John had expected something else of the Messiah. He had evidently expected the Messiah to execute God's final judgment, to end evil immediately, and to bring paradise upon earth. He commissioned two of his disciples to go and question Jesus (v.19). Jesus was not insensitive to John's question nor resentful of what may seem to be doubt. He had committed himself to the kind of a Messiah he would be and his actions were consistent with his intentions. John's disciples were advised to tell him how the Messiah was using his power to help people. That was to be proof to him.

Do not minimize your words and actions. Make your real self known to others through them.

THE NAME OF THE GAME

Luke 7:24–35

What kind of a game is life? How can we understand what is going on? People want to know what things mean.

John's disciples had watched Jesus use his power to help people and had gone back to tell John what they had seen.

Jesus talked to the crowd then about John the Baptist. They needed to understand some things about John. They were not to take him lightly. He was not just a distraction like a plant shaking in the wind (v.24). Nor was he to be taken as a vain spectacle like gorgeous apparel (v.25). He was a prophet and more (v.26). Jesus quoted Scripture, Malachi 3:1, to help them understand the great role of John. John was the messenger that had been promised to prepare the way for the Messiah. No other man before Christ had a greater role to fill. After saying that, Jesus made a statement that must have been beyond the comprehension of the crowd. Even though John was the greatest of the prophets, he was less than the least in the kingdom of God (v.28).

The greatest privilege a person can have is to be a follower of Jesus.

People did not all respond the same to John and to Jesus. What was the meaning of their varied reactions? Jesus said people were like children who couldn't decide whether to play wedding or funeral (v.32). They also couldn't decide what kind of religious life-style to admire. They said John had a devil and they criticized him because he was unsociable (v.33). On the other hand they criticized Jesus because he had a zest for life and enjoyed being with people (v.34).

The game of life cannot make sense to people until they have turned to God for wisdom. God is able to use a wide variety of personalities to accomplish his purpose.

Understanding the meaning of life can reinforce one's commitment.

ONE'S CAPACITY FOR LOVE

Luke 7:36–50

Do some have a greater ability to love than others? How is one's ability to love related to his need for love?

Some people invite Jesus to be with them but they do not really want him. An example was a Pharisee who asked Jesus to eat with him (v.36). The dinner was in the open courtyard where people could stroll in. They lay on couches at the table. A woman of the street came up to him (v.37) and wept and her tears fell on his feet (v.38). She wiped them with her hair and poured perfume on them. The Pharisee jumped to the conclusion that Jesus was naive and didn't know the kind of woman she was (v.39).

Jesus understood more than the Pharisee. He asked him who would love his creditor most, a debtor forgiven a sizable amount or one forgiven ten times as much. Simon, the Pharisee, responded that surely one who was forgiven the most would love the most (v.43). With such an answer, how could he miss the point! How blind is smugness! Jesus reminded Simon that even though he had invited Jesus, he had not extended the least courtesy of welcome (v.44). Can it be possible that we are like Simon the Pharisee? Do we pass up opportunities to show our love for Jesus?

Simon the Pharisee did not really love Jesus. He only wanted the prestige of being associated with him. But he wouldn't give to him one evidence of love.

On the other hand was the sinful woman. Jesus had forgiven her of her sins. He had cleansed her heart and made her a new person. Instead of despising herself she had a new sense of worth. No longer was she filled with shame; she was filled with joy and love. All she had was a little perfume in a container around her neck. She emptied it with love on her Savior's feet. He said to her, "Your faith has saved you; go in peace" (v.50).

UNIT
4

Making the Most of Means

Idealists will ask, "Why?" Realists will ask, "How?" Many have dreamed great dreams but could not command the means for accomplishment. The greatest dream or purpose is that which Christians have. To carry out their intentions they must learn to make the most of means.

Much of the work of Christians is with people and therefore depends upon the responsiveness of hearers. Witnessing and teaching are like sowing seed. The seed of the gospel should be sown in the hearing of all kinds of people. The variety of responses will be a result of a variety of factors. One of the most important factors will be the very nature of the hearers. A worker should, therefore, make the best use of means but keep in mind that responses will vary with persons.

Think what potential is in human abilities if these could be directed into the full service of God. But man is wasting his means. On one hand he is exhausting natural resources. On the other he is ignoring and neglecting his own personal resources. People destroy themselves by various indulgences.

Man's life has an end. Some may dread that end so much they lose their effectiveness for good. The dread of death may be relieved by faith in Christ. In him death becomes properly related to life. Death is the end of one's earthly assignment; it is a release from life's problems; it is fulfilment of true individuality; it is the opening door for union with loved ones, God's servants, and Christ himself. Death cannot be as grim as it seems in view of the fact that Jesus can overpower it and restore life. One's view of death may even motivate him in the best use of life's resources.

Means should be properly related to mission. One should not lose sight of his assignment in the effort to provide facilities and improve abilities for his mission. To keep mission and means well balanced one should be receptive and responsive to the leadership of Christ.

Means and end should not be confused. Living one's life is not an end but a means. Life may be thought of as a commodity. What will you buy with your life? Will you use it to accumulate a quantity of goods? Or will you use it and all you might accumulate as a means of bringing a great gift of loving service to God.

Reinforcement for one's commitment may come from seeing how his mission fits into the total plan of God. This calls for a knowledge of what has been done in the past and an understanding of the purpose of God.

Why should men of today use their tremendous new power in serving God? It would be easy to answer that they should do so in order to be the greatest generation of all history. But that may not be a possibility. A future generation will likely exceed this one. The greatest motivation is to understand that Christ is so involved in this world that we can see him in every needy situation and respond immediately as an expression of love to him.

Polarization of people and the intolerance of diversity threaten to divide Christians and set them against each other. The possibility is that Christians will turn their means to the establishing of superiority over each other rather than to service to God.

Chapters 8 and 9 of Luke will help us think of the best use of means.

THE USE OF OPPORTUNITIES

Luke 8:1–15

Occasionally, ideas come from persons with means. However, in some instances persons with means have been challenged to support ideas beyond those of their own. In this way they have tried to make the most of their means.

Jesus permitted those who followed him to support his work. Luke listed the names of several women who ministered to him and his disciples out of their means (v.2–3).

Not everyone who had the opportunity responded to Jesus in the same way. The variety of responses was compared by Jesus to different kinds of ground. There is ground that is hard as a roadway and, of course, seed can't sprout there (v.5). Some ground is only shallow soil and cannot sustain growth for long (v.6). Some ground is already crowded with weeds and good seed is choked and crowded out (v.7). However, some ground is good and very productive (v.8). The meaning of the parable is clear to us because we know its explanation.

The disciples asked Jesus what the parable meant. He explained that the kinds of soil represented kinds of hearers. Some do not respond at all. Some respond but not with depth of commitment. Some respond but with such reservation that they do not really make growing room in their lives for the gospel (vv.12–14). However, some respond in such a manner that they become fully productive for Christ (v.15).

Today's Christians could make better use of their means to proclaim the gospel. Great dreamers are needed to envision giant steps to take in witnessing for Christ and to plan for massive ministry efforts. These ideas will need the full response of persons with means and resources. People are needed who will be responsive and productive like good soil.

Let us be receptive to the gospel message and responsive to its call to service.

THE USE OF ABILITY

Luke 8:16–25

Let a person look to see what he has that he can use for good.

One thing that can be used for good is influence. Influence is like a light. It is effective if used properly. One should not hide his light (v.16). Instead he should share the news of the good life that he has in Christ. This may seem to some to be a risk to one's peace of mind and good relations. However this is a time for risking. Risk-oriented persons will explore the solar system, will conquer man's physical ills, will help solve social and political problems, and will proclaim the gospel in the face of all obstacles.

What does it mean to give yourself fully to the service of Christ? What would it mean to "do your thing" for God? Jesus was intensely occupied with helping people. His mother and brothers sought him, evidently to caution him (v.19). Hearing of their concern Jesus said that his true kindred were those who heard the word of God and did it (v.21). Christianity calls for a person to do things. It is Bible based, Christ directed, church oriented, action inducing, Spirit powered, and aimed at good results. One's response to God's word in active service overshadows all other relational obligations.

Life will have its storms that will threaten ventures and hopes. Sometimes these may be more than one can withstand. Resources may be inadequate. The storms may be ill health, suffering, grief, fear, sorrow, resentment, and despair. In the storm the disciples faced, they called on Jesus (v.24) and he rebuked the wind and waves and things were calm. Christ is the ultimate resource. His ability is available to those who call on him.

In trouble, call upon Christ. He can help in every problem of life. Let us then follow his example and use our ability also for good.

49

RECLAIMING WASTED HUMANITY

Luke 8:26–39

The greatest waste of all is wasted humanity. Not only does man pollute and destroy his world but he also pollutes and destroys his own mind, heart, and personality.

When Jesus came into the country of the Gadarenes he was met by a man who was a social reject (v.27). The man could not stand people nor their restraints or even customs. He lived in tombs. His tension increased to its maximum when he met Jesus. It was torment, and he cried to Jesus in anguish (v.28). This man is almost like a caricature of some people today. There are those who want to live only with the past and are unable to enjoy happy meaningful association with others. They may even seem to have strength but it is wasted instead of being well used.

Here was a man whose life was so fragmented and filled with evil spirits that he called himself Legion (v.30). He was a problem to his family and a danger to anyone within reach. What can be done about the great waste of humanity?

Jesus healed the man. Luke reported the strange disposal of the devils in the man. They left the man and entered a large herd of swine nearby (v.32). The evil in this one man was enough to drive 2,000 swine crazy.

Word of the miracle spread. The curious crowded out to see what had happened. They found the man, clothed and sane, sitting and listening to Jesus (v.35).

Do people really want to see wasted humanity saved? The Gadarenes were frightened when they saw the man whom Jesus healed. They even asked Jesus to leave their country (v.37).

As Jesus prepared to leave, he told the man to show others what God had done for him (v.39).

Share with others the good news of how God has blessed you.

CHRIST THE ULTIMATE RESOURCE

Luke 8:40–56

Life's grimmest threat is death. It's coming. It will take loved ones from us and it will take us from them. Can nothing be done about this fatal finality? At the best, scientific wonders only postpone the inevitable.

Hope is added to our lives by the response of Jesus to Jairus. Something really can be done. In the presence of death one can turn to Jesus. Jairus came to Jesus about his dying daughter (v.41).

An amazing incident happened as Jesus was on the way to Jairus' home. A crowd pressed about him. In a sense every person around him was lost in the crowd. However, one in the crowd had great need, a woman who had been hemorrhaging for twelve years (v.43) She touched Jesus and was healed. He asked for her to reveal herself. At first she was afraid but then told how she had been healed (v.47). Jesus immediately encouraged Jairus and told him to believe and to have hope (v.50). He spoke reassurance to those gathered in Jairus' home (v.52). He advised them that the girl was not dead but asleep. Those who heard this laughed in scorn. They knew the girl was dead (v.53). What a difference in viewpoints and in conclusions! The world may despair at death but Christians are taught by their Master to have confidence that death will be terminated by an awakening.

Jesus called out to the dead girl to arise (v.54). Life returned to her and Jesus told her parents to feed her (v.55). The miraculous does not eliminate the need for the mundane. The ultimate resource is Christ but instead of overruling man's efforts he makes a place for man to respond with his own resources and deeds.

You can count on it. Try and see.

51

MEANS AND MINISTRY

Luke 9:1–17

The mission that God gives to Christians is impossible except as Christ gives the means for its accomplishment.

Jesus had an assignment for the twelve that would demand more of them than they had. He shared with them his own power and authority (v.1). They had a message to deliver to people and a ministry to render. They were to preach that God rules and they were to help people. This was primarily a mission of service but it was also a training experience. They were to understand that an overconcentration on means could be an encumbrance (v.3). Jesus spoke also about the propriety of the Christian messenger depending on his hearers for support and help (v.4). Their mission was a success. Word of it reached even Herod the ruler and his conscience was disturbed because of his killing of John the Baptist (v.7).

When the twelve returned, Jesus took them to an uninhabited area evidently for rest. But people sought him out. He was always accessible to people who wanted him. He talked to them about how God rules and he healed those who needed it (v.11). He was interrupted by the twelve as evening came. They advised him to dismiss the crowd so the people could hunt lodging and food. Jesus responded as a good host and told his followers to feed the crowd. Almost in shock they reported their food inventory to Jesus. It was hardly enough for one person (v.13). Undismayed Jesus told how the crowd should be grouped, took the meager supply of food, prayed, broke the food into pieces, and gave it to the disciples to distribute. He was their new Moses and had full command of divine providence. Everyone was satisfied and baskets of food were left.

Share in the concern of Christ for the physical needs of people and also for their need to respond to the rule of God.

THE MASTER OF MEN AND THEIR MEANS

Luke 9:18–27

What you think may be more important than you realize. Ideas, concepts, and understanding—these are the basis for all actions and for life itself. What do people think of Jesus? Do you know? This is an important question. Jesus asked it of his disciples (v.18). When they had responded, he then asked, "Who do you think I am?" (v.20), that is the real question. Jesus immediately cautioned his followers about discussing that publicly then (v.21). He was fully committed to the suffering that must come and his followers needed to understand its necessity (v.22). The success he anticipated could come only after his suffering.

This look into the immediate future must have been alarming to the disciples. Jesus utilized their concern to call for deeper commitment. A follower of Jesus would need to be able to turn away from personal desire (v.23). His cross was a daily giving of his life in following Christ. The surest way to lose life is to restrict it by barricades of fear and within walls of selfishness (v.24). Gains in this world are temporal. They are nontransferable (v.25). One's value system should be tuned with that which is eternal and enduring.

Of what are you proud? Or ashamed? If you can answer this question honestly, you may have a good measurement of the genuineness of your Christian faith. How can God tolerate someone who is ashamed of Jesus (v.26)? But then that person will not even want to face God, will he?

What would it be like to live continually under the rule and guidance of God? Jesus said that some of his hearers would see the kingdom of God before they died (v.27). This statement has been a puzzle to many. Was Jesus perhaps teaching that the full rule of God may be an experience even in this life?

Lose your life for God; spend it with abandon in his service.

53

HERITAGE MAY BE A HELP

Luke 9:28–36

The "here and now" is not all that there is. It is hardly true to say the past is gone and the future has not come and therefore all that is real is the present. The present moment has meaning beyond that put into it by those living it.

Jesus had led his disciples to an affirmation of his messiahship. The next step was divine confirmation of Peter's great confession. A week later Jesus took the three disciples in the inner circle, Peter, James, and John, up a mountain to pray (v.28). Something happened there that was supernatural. The countenance of Jesus was changed (v.29). He did not look the same. His divine identity became apparent.

The true nature of Jesus was related to the work that God had been doing all through man's long history. The message of Moses and the commitment of Elijah were relevant to Jesus and also to us. Those men were not ancient heros who just as well have never lived as far as Jesus was concerned or as far as we are concerned. They are God's messengers who served in their day, who stood by Jesus (v.30), and who have a word for us.

Jesus talked with them about his coming death (v.31).

Peter and his companions had been very sleepy, but they awoke and saw Jesus in his glory and the two who stood with him (v.32). What a sight for mortal eyes to see! Peter, who did not need understanding in order to speak, proposed that three shrines be erected, one for Jesus, one for Moses, and one for Elijah (v.33). A cloud came over them and a voice spoke that seemed to correct Peter. Try reading verse 35 aloud and emphasize the words "this" and "him." *"This* is my beloved Son: hear *him."* God himself spoke and identified his Son. He then charged the followers of Jesus to hear him.

Find strength from God's messengers for the mission ahead of us. Most of all, though, listen to Christ Jesus.

COMPETENCE IN CRISES

Luke 9:37–45

Emergencies and crises confront one at every step. Only briefly can one withdraw for spiritual experiences of infilling and reinforcement. You just can't stay on a mountaintop long.

When Jesus came down from the mountain where he had been transfigured, he was met by a man with an epileptic son (v.38). The boy was being knocked about by the evil spirit of this disease as though a boxer were battering him to the ground (v.39). It was heartbreaking. The disciples were pressured both by their own compassion and by the man's plea to do something, but they were helpless (v.40). A hazard in being a Christian is that people may expect you to duplicate the works of Christ. A disorderly crowd had gathered and things in general were out of control. The competence of Christ in a crisis was seen again. First he rebuked the crowd. They were not learning what he had tried to teach them (v.41). As the boy was brought, he had another violent spell and Jesus healed him (v.42). Christ was not powerless. Nor are men of today; they can duplicate with their science almost every wonderful healing miracle Christ performed with supernatural power. Let modern men have the Spirit of Christ. Let them hear the cries of the needy and respond with their great abilities. Christ would do it. He put ministry to people's needs ahead of everything else even though he knew such commitment would end on a cross.

Luke drew a remarkable parallel. He said that Jesus delivered the child to his father. Then he quoted Jesus as admonishing his followers that he himself would be delivered into the hands of his enemies (v.44). They sensed a foreboding in the mind of Jesus. Their fear silenced them.

Can you see both the needs around you and also your own limitations? Will you do all that you can do and also resort to the great competence of Christ?

REWARDS AND INVESTMENTS

Luke 9:46–62

What can following Jesus mean to people of today? Can serving him be an investment with eternal significance?

As Jesus' mind was turning more toward the cross, an argument arose among his disciples about which of them would be greatest (v.46). They were dealing with the problem of their own motivation. Jesus set a child in their midst (v.42). He then advised them to be motivated by looking for him and finding him in every situation of need. Love a child in the name of Jesus and you love Jesus (v.48). It is in exalting others that one becomes great.

Some might say that it is important to know who your enemies are. One might be motivated by opposition if nothing else. If that is so, Christians need to be careful or they may waste their strength fighting the wrong foe. John told Jesus about a stranger doing good things in Jesus' name. John and others stopped him because he did not belong to their group (v.49). Some Christians in their zeal have turned to attack fellow Christians over processes and opinions. Jesus advised John not to hinder the man (v.50).

Jesus approached a Samaritan village on his way to Jerusalem and committed to some messengers the task of entering the town and securing arrangements (v.52). The townspeople would not receive him because he was on his way to Jerusalem (v.53). What opportunities are prevented by prejudice! James and John were furious and asked him to burn the town down (v.54). Jesus said they didn't realize what spirit was motivating them (v.55).

Three men in succession asked about investing their lives with him. He advised them he had no material gain to give and he expected total commitment from them.

Set your eyes on Christ and commit yourself decisively to be true to him in your every circumstance.

UNIT
5
Philosophy of Life

Life has become increasingly complex and it cannot be lived satisfactorily in a haphazard way. By what principles shall modern man live? Everyone has principles to guide him whether he recognizes them or not. These form his philosophy of life. A person may have a view of life worked out thoughtfully with causes and ends in mind. However, most people probably have only vague concepts that they have not analyzed or intelligently accepted. The Gospel of Luke can be helpful to a person in clarifying his philosophy of life. The next two chapters of Luke (10–11) may be helpful in the development of principles to live by.

Philosophy is concerned with what is real, what is valuable, and what can be known and how.

Life can be a great mission. It can be the realization of the kingdom of God. That may sound like an oversimplification. If that is the case, perhaps it should be repeated in slightly different words. Growing in accepting the rule of God is what life is all about. Recognizing the reality of the will of God helps one to establish his set of values. One's values determine what he is and what he will become. Rejection of God has more practical results than most people understand. It amounts to a rejection of such principles and values of life that deterioration and destruction are inevitable.

Life at its best is filled with happiness. The search of the centuries has been to discover the secret of happiness. For some happiness may be survival; for some, security; for some, sufficiency; for some, success; for some, service. But, greatest of all, happiness is salvation. True joy is closely related to ultimate truth. Coming to know eternal truth is an experience in ecstasy. This truth does not come though by exploration and discovery. It comes by Christ Jesus revealing God to us.

The greatest thing in life is love. What more is there than loving God and loving one's neighbor? Don't get "hung up" though on who your neighbor is. That isn't really the question. The question is who will be a neighbor to those who suffer and are in need. Will you volunteer? By the way, when it comes to love, actions speak louder than words. But being present is the best of all—take a tip from Mary, Martha's sister.

Prayer needs to be a continuing life activity. Jesus prayed. So should we. Prayer is convenient but it isn't easy. It is a Christian skill that calls for much practice. While a person should not hesitate to pray for things, he should most of all pray for an awareness of the presence of God.

Can the Christian philosopher explain the presence of suffering and evil? Christ did not ignore nor seek to explain away the bad elements of life. He cast the devil out of the diseased and the oppressed and he made life worth living. The devil is no match for Christ. In Christ a person can experience wholeness. Evil is like darkness; it retreats in the presence of light. A life made whole by Christ is full and has no room in it for evil. A person must strive for complete honesty if he would be whole.

The study of Luke 10 and 11 will reinforce your Christian commitment and growth.

THE REAL KINGDOM

Luke 10:1–16

A person needs to be related to a venture that is a significant part of life itself. He needs to find his place in the work of God.

Jesus had successfully sent out the twelve on a mission of preaching and ministry. After awhile he followed that with the launching of a mission involving seventy disciples (v.1). They were to be advance agents going to places Jesus intended to visit. They were to go as teams of two reinforcing the testimony of each other. Jesus saw people as a ripe harvest. His disciples were laborers gathering in the harvest (v.2). Jesus told his followers that they were going out like lambs among wolves (v.3). The "seventy" were to go with a sense of urgency. They were to search out hearers who wanted peace. They were to accept whatever hospitality was offered.

Their mission was to heal and preach. Their message was singular. They were to announce that the rule of God was increasingly becoming a reality. It was getting closer to them (v.9). The world exists that people might be brought under the benevolent rule of God. Although people may be like a ripe harvest, they are not like passive grain. They may resist the very person seeking to lead them to salvation. The messenger of Christ should expect opposition and hindrances. But he should remember that the kingdom of God is real. Established cities have perished but God's rule will endure forever (vv.12–13). These cities have a greater hope, though, for God's favor in judgment than does a person rejecting the word of Jesus' followers. The Christian who recognizes this can understand how serious his testimony is. The person who hears him hears Christ. The person who rejects him rejects Christ.

Nothing is more real than the kingdom of God. Do you realize it?

59

TRUE JOY AND ULTIMATE TRUTH

Luke 10:17–24

Ancient philosophers sought the greatest good, or the *summum bonum*. Some felt it was happiness. But how could happiness be attained? Through indulgence or self-control?

When the "seventy" returned from their mission, they were elated over their success (v.17). Jesus cautioned them about what to rejoice over. Our source of true joy should not be what we do but what has been done for us (v.20). God's work in and upon us is our salvation and therefore the occasion for real happiness.

Let men who are conquering the universe realize that, as important as that is, it is not comparable to becoming rightly related to God. Joy comes from being sure your name is on God's list.

The wisest men have sought to know the ultimate truth. What is the world? What is life? What is the purpose of man? Is there a God and can human creatures know him? There is truth to be known that men cannot discover. They can receive it only by revelation. Such truth can come to a child or to the simple as well as to the learned (v.21). The condition for receiving this revelation of ultimate truth is twofold: first must be the will of God and then must be the responsiveness of man.

Jesus made a claim no one else would dare to make. He said God the Father knew his true identity and that he knew the Father and would reveal him to whomever he wished (v.22). If you want to know the truth, that is, if you want to know God, then come to know Jesus. In him you meet and commune with God. In Christ God comes among us. That is what the prophets wanted to see—the manifestation of God on the earth (v.24). Christ is that manifestation. He is the point toward which all history moved and all history flows.

Be willing to accept the truth and you will know it.

THE HIGHEST VALUES

Luke 10:25–42

If a person were to have eternal life, what kind of life would it be? Shouldn't one be concerned as much about the quality of life as about its duration?

A lawyer asked Jesus what to do to secure eternal life (v.25). Jesus asked what the law said (v.26). This legal expert quoted from Deuteronomy 6:4–5 and Leviticus 19:18. Love God with your whole being and love your neighbor as yourself (v.27).

The lawyer felt he was being made to look foolish. It was obvious that he was not living up to his best knowledge. He could not question the command to love God. Therefore, he challenged Jesus to explain the second command. Who is a person's neighbor (v.29)? In answer Jesus told the story that has been called "The Good Samaritan." He described people passing a man who had been robbed and left half dead (vv.30–32). Why do people pass others in need? Some want to leave ministry to institutions. Some fear to help others because of the risk and liability. Some do not have time or money. Jesus told of a man who helped in spite of racial and social barriers (v.33). The helper spent time, effort, and money and obligated himself to go further (vv. 34–35). Then Jesus asked a strange question. "Who was the needy man's neighbor?" My question should not be, "What kind of a person should I help?" but, "Am I the kind of a person who helps others?"

Philosophy has to do with viewpoints and values. How might these be tested? They could be tested in practical experience. For instance, what if Jesus came into your home. Would you scurry like Martha to do all kinds of personal favors for him (vv.40–41)? He doesn't need such favors. He would be pleased if we, like Mary, chose to sit close to him and learn what he wants to teach us (v.42).

Nothing is worth as much as love. Give it.

IS PRAYER REAL?

Luke 11:1–13

In fantasy people have dreamed of being granted their wishes. Even Christians have wondered if they might get anything they wanted by asking properly.

As Jesus was praying, his disciples asked him to teach them to pray (v.1). Here is Luke's version of "The Lord's Prayer." How shall it be viewed? Prayer must be based on an awareness of God as Father (v.2). God is holy and he can't be tricked into becoming involved in unworthy enterprises. How should one talk to God? First of all, get in step with him. Lay aside selfishness and pray, "Thy kingdom come." Does this mean that a person shouldn't pray for anything for himself? Why, no! He can ask for material needs to be met. He can ask for forgiveness and receive it just as he practices it. He can also recognize his tendency to do things he shouldn't and ask for help to avoid situations with which he can't cope.

Do you pray persistently or do you give up easily? This question is not meant to imply that God is hardhearted. He is not. He is most generous. He delights in aiding persons. For various reasons he may not answer prayers immediately. Persistent praying may be a help to believers in growing. It may also help them see their error if they are not praying right. Furthermore, it may increase their anticipation so that God's response becomes an even greater blessing.

What is prayer? It is asking. It is seeking. It is knocking. The person praying must be more serious about it than a lot of people realize.

To pray is like a child asking his loving father for that which he needs. The greatest need that we have as God's children is a real awareness of his presence. God can be trusted to answer our prayer.

Let us ask for the Holy Spirit and be assured of God's response.

THE REALITY OF EVIL

Luke 11:14–26

To some the idea of a devil seems fantastic. However, they cannot deny the reality of evil. It operates paradoxically as the work of an irrational intelligence. Jesus described the working of evil in personal terms.

When he healed a dumb man, the crowd said he did it because he had authority from the prince of devils to cast out devils (v.15). The people of that day had practically no understanding of the causes of catastrophe and disaster. The most powerful force in their lives was that of evil. In their minds the only thing that could overthrow evil would be a devil with authority over evil. Jesus responded to their charge by saying that the devil was shrewd enough not to fight against himself (v.18). He showed them the absurdity of their argument by pointing out that it would imply that every person overthrowing evil could do it only if he were in league with the devil (v.19). Then he described his action as being evidence of the finger of God (v.20). The rule of God was being extended to them. They should have realized that Christ was strong enough to expel the evil from any life. (vv.21–22).

Life is more, though, than being purged of the bad. One cannot be neutral in the struggle between good and evil. People in our times must realize that moral neutrality is a vote for wickedness. A life is like a house; it can accommodate an occupant. Who will live in you—God or the devil? This challenge may be startling. Jesus told of a man who got rid of an unclean spirit but he didn't replace it with anything good (v.24). When the evil spirit saw the emptiness of the man's life, he enlisted seven spirits worse than himself and moved back in (vv.25–26). What a horror story!

Be so filled with the Holy Spirit that there will be no emptiness in your life.

63

THE POSSIBILITY OF WHOLENESS

Luke 11:27–36

Sometimes life seems to consist of a bunch of pieces that are not related. People may act wrongly as a result of having only partial information. They may also fail to measure up to life's full potential and settle for an existence that is only a fraction of what it could be.

One way in which people fail is to draw wrong conclusions or to make false judgments. Some of these may seem fairly harmless. For instance, a woman in a crowd called out to Jesus that it would have been wonderful to have been his mother (v.27). This bit of sentimentality was spoken on an emotional impulse. It was meant as a compliment but it was not valid. Jesus corrected her. The most wonderful thing in life is to hear and respond to the word of God (v.28). The place of Mary the mother of Jesus is no greater than that of any person who does the will of God.

The growing crowd asked for a sign and Jesus resisted the pressure to perform for the curious. He said that the only real sign would be the sign of Jonah (v.29). This was a reference to the resurrection and no one needs more than that to be convinced that Jesus is the Christ. Then he spoke of Solomon and of Jonah. The greatest wisdom of antiquity and the most effective preaching of all time were nothing compared to Jesus. The Queen of Sheba and the Ninevites were qualified to condemn those who rejected Jesus (vv.31–32).

Men needed light not a sign. God had given men light and he had not concealed it (v.33). But, what good is light if one closes his eyes? The eye then is a lamp to the body (v.34). This means that only by being willing to accept the truth can a person benefit by it. The next question, then, is how much will he let the truth affect him. He can be whole only as he lets the light of God fill his inner being (v.36).

Live a full whole life. Christ will help you do it.

UNMASKING THE FALSE

Luke 11:37–54

Truth cannot exist side by side with the false. Jesus could accommodate himself to the ignorance and weakness of people. However, he refused to tolerate hypocrisy.

A Pharisee invited Jesus home to eat. Jesus came to the table without washing his hands (v.38). He observed the Pharisee's questioning look and took the opportunity to denounce the religious leaders. With their authority and power they had lost sight of what was really important in life. They had magnified regulations and processes above righteousness and persons.

Jesus said the Pharisees were concerned about clean cups and plates but not about lives of goodness and purity (v.39). If one gives attention to the inner life, other matters will take their rightful place.

Then Jesus made six indictments against the religious leaders around him. Each charge begins with "Woe unto you."

He charged the Pharisees with being more concerned about giving God every tenth vegetable out of their gardens than about giving him their love and serving him with righteous lives (v.42). Tithing is proper but it needs to be practiced with love. He also accused the Pharisees of having a passion for prestige and recognition (v.43). He said the scribes and Pharisees were hypocrites (v.44). They put on a good appearance but corrupted everyone near them.

He charged the lawyers with adding burdensome regulations to people already breaking down; with honoring dead prophets and harassing living ones; and with knowing the truth and preventing people from learning it (vv.46–52).

Filled with anger his opponents increased the pressure on him hoping to trap and destroy him.

Live in honesty and truthfulness. That's really the only way a person can tolerate himself.

The Possibility
of Failure

To say we have nothing to fear but fear itself is a bold slogan. It may be a challenging rally cry for a nation going to war but it isn't a realistic assessment of life.

One should understand that failure is a possibility. One's whole life even can be a failure. Surely this is to be feared. Failure may range from blighted lives and broken homes to a bankrupt nation and a warring world. All around us is failure. Success is not an inevitability in any life. For a matter of fact, in some instances failure must come before success can be realized. Worst of all, some persons may fail life and continue their failure eternally.

In chapters 12 and 13 of Luke we find instances that encourage us to be cautious and also words of actual warning. The day in which we live is a sophisticated time in which people are advised not to fear. They are told in various ways that fear is unnecessary and that they should overcome it. The wise course would be to recognize that failure and ruin are possibilities but to have the faith that enables one to live in courage and hope. A courageous man once marked the word "failure" out of his dictionary. Such determination is commendable, but it still does not guarantee that one will experience nothing but success. However, a person can live with courage who has Christ in his heart and who depends on the leadership of the Holy Spirit.

Many think that the surest way to prevent failure is to have wealth. The idea of our materialistic philosophy is that money can buy almost anything. Money does offer certain power and privileges. However, the person who depends upon material goods for security and success is vulnerable at a number of points. Unforseen circumstances can ruin his hopes at any time and failure can be the result.

A person has the greatest peace of mind if he lives in constant readiness to give an account of his life to God. Life is not an accident for anyone. It is a trust from God. He expects something from every person and holds him responsible for all he does. Judgment goes on continually in some ways. We are tested every day. However, a final judgment is to be faced. This we can count on.

A person's life will be judged and his fate will be determined on the basis of what he has done. Every reasonable person should accept this possibility and should recognize that he could lose in the final judgment. This is cause enough to fear and therefore repent.

In the long run life will be judged to be a failure or a success depending upon its relationship to the kingdom of God. Only by coming under the rule of God can one have eternal hope. Christ is the way. No one can come to the Father but by him. To reject him is to reject the One who sent him.

FEAR AND COURAGE

Luke 12:1–12

A part of wisdom is knowing what to fear. Only the naive would insist that there is nothing to fear. In some ways the early Christians had more to fear than anyone.

The crowds around Jesus were increasing so much that people were stepping on one another. Even with this he spoke primarily to his disciples (v.1). His time was running out and he had much to say to them. For one thing they were to be suspicious of the Pharisees and not to be fooled by them (v.2). They were to fear their hypocrisy. This did not mean that they were to silence their testimony. They were just to remember that whatever they said in the dark or in the light, in narrow halls or from the housetops would be repeated everywhere (v.3). They were not to live in fear of death. Men could kill them but couldn't send them to hell (vv.4–5). They were to fear God and to remember that he had even numbered the hairs of their head (v.7). How real the presence of God became as Christ spoke!

Jesus advised his followers that they should acknowledge him before men if they were counting on him some day acknowledging them before the angels of God (v.9). Can you envision Christ stepping up to your side and saying to all of his angels, "This is one of my followers"?

Another thing to fear, said Jesus, was blasphemy against the Holy Spirit (v.10). Cutting the Holy Spirit out of your life is spiritual suicide. It is like spinning out of orbit and plunging into outer space.

The person though who relies on the Holy Spirit will not even need to fear when facing trial and death for his faith. He can be assured that the Holy Spirit will give him at that very time what he is to say (vv.11–12).

Be wise enough to be afraid of that which you should fear. Then trust the Lord for courage.

THE TROUBLE WITH WEALTH

Luke 12:13–34

From time to time someone criticizes riches as though there were something wrong with prosperity. Is it wrong to be affluent? What is the trouble with wealth?

A man spoke up from the crowd and asked Jesus to order his brother to divide his inheritance with him (v.13). Jesus refused to get involved in this family squabble. He spoke further to the crowd warning them against covetousness (v.15). Life is more than having a bank account. Then he told them about a rich man's continued prosperity (v.16). His increased wealth was a problem to him. He debated with himself about what he should do (v.17). Note that he didn't ask the poor and starving nor the victims of catastrophe what he should do. He didn't even ask God. His decision was to build larger storehouses and to retire (vv.18–19). He should have realized that food is for stomachs and not for barns. Security is a natural desire but it is not to be had at the deprivation of others. He had concern only for himself. See how many times "I" and "my" occur in verses 17–19. The man thought he had years left when he had only one night. Laying up treasure for oneself cannot compare to gaining the riches of God (v.21).

Then Jesus talked directly with his disciples. They were not to let their lives be ruined by worry to preserve them (vv.22–23). This does not condone irresponsibility or heedlessness. It calls for one to be aware of the providential factor of life. Birds and flowers are under the care of God and so are people (vv.24–28). Jesus even said that to worry was to be worldly rather than Christian (v.30). A person's search should be to do the will of God (v.31). Jesus said, "Fear not, little flock."

Put your treasure where your heart is or your treasure will kidnap your heart (v.34).

BE READY

Luke 12:35–48

Things will end some day. This may be like the sudden coming of inspectors to examine the quality of your work. Will you be ready? This is a little bit like a military camp being on constant alert.

Jesus advised his hearers to keep in working condition and to be ready for the coming of their Lord (v.35). They should be like workers expecting their supervisor to come at any moment (v.36). How good it would be if he could come and find them working so hard that he would relieve them for rest by taking their place himself (v.37). That seems like a dream too good to be true but it could be. Many people live without thought that they will ever have to give an account of their life accomplishments. They act like there is no need to hurry about doing good. What difference will it make a hundred years from now? Who will ever judge them to determine whether they lived right and well or not? The very point that Jesus was making was that life is serious and that each person is responsible and must sometime give an account of himself to God.

Peter may have felt a little guilty and he asked if what Jesus was saying applied to the disciples only or to everyone (v.41). It is interesting that in response to Peter Jesus spoke pointedly about servants with authority over other servants. Misused authority was evidently a great problem in that day (vv.45–46). It continues to be a problem in our highly complex society. What strange things can happen to a person who gets a little power.

Jesus told them clearly that punishment would be given to those who deserved it and that an evil person who knew better would be punished more than one who didn't (vv.47–48).

Be sure you know what God expects of you and get busy doing it. He is watching.

THE CERTAINTY OF JUDGMENT

Luke 12:49–59

Various kinds of opportunities depend upon examinations. Sometimes a candidate for a position will study books and practice diligently in order to qualify. This is commendable. How much more ought we as Christians prepare for the opportunities for service we face on earth and also for the ultimate judgment.

Jesus was quite concerned about the problems in the immediate future. He had referred to judgment and then he said he had come to bring it, to throw fire on the earth (v.49). Remember that John the Baptist had foretold that Christ would baptize with the Holy Spirit and with fire (v.16). The next words imply that this was not to come until after a coming experience of Jesus. He said he yet had to experience a baptism by which he must have meant his suffering and death (v.50). What he went through! The tension within him was mounting. He could foresee that division rather than peace would be precipitated by his life (v.51). The closest of human relationships would be disrupted as people chose sides for and against Christ. Households would be divided (v.52). Parents against children with even the in-laws taking sides (v.53). The division of a family is a tragedy but its union in Christ is a foretaste of heaven.

The immediate response of people was normal. They wanted to know when these things would take place. Jesus reminded them how they endeavored to become skilled at predicting the weather. He said they should try harder to understand the times (v.56).

Then with a reference to the fate of a debtor Jesus advised his hearers that it would be wise to pay their debt to God without delay (vv.57–59).

Wouldn't it be foolish to go to court against God? Consider what you owe him and settle quickly. Be wise.

REPENT OR PERISH

Luke 13:1–9

Are the victims of tragedy unusually wicked people? That sounds like a foolish question. We would have to answer and say, "Of course not!" Perhaps, though, the news of a catastrophe or disaster should not be passed over too lightly. Would we be wise to take it as a warning?

Some arrived in Jesus' presence and reported to him the horrible news of Pilate's soldiers killing a bunch of Galileans even as they were worshiping (v.1). They may have told it with the thought that these people deserved what they got or else God would have prevented it. Jesus denied that these were greater sinners than their neighbors (v.2) and then he warned his hearers that they could suffer the same or worse fate. He said their only hope was to repent (v.3). Some may have thought this was a political warning. Rebellion was in the heart of nearly every Jew, especially the Galileans. If Pilate would kill some of the rebellious, then all of the others were in jeopardy. They should change their attitudes and ways or they would all perish. Jesus then referred to eighteen who were killed by the fall of the tower at Siloam (v.4). Here was a calamity at Jerusalem that took innocent lives. Jesus used the news of this event also to warn his hearers. The warning was simple: repent or perish (v.5). Christians through the centuries have looked on these warnings as having spiritual significance. They have witnessed to others that a life without Christ terminates as an ultimate disaster in eternal punishment and that the only escape is repentance and faith.

Then Jesus told of an unfruitful fig tree that was ordered destroyed but was given one more year because of the caretaker's request (vv.6–9). That fig tree could represent Jerusalem or anyone living on borrowed time.

What use will you make of the time left?

TIME TO DO GOOD

Luke 13:10–17

Is it ever out of place to do good for someone? In our time conscious and highly regulated society we might think of instances when we would not do certain good things because of tradition or rules. In this technological age are we as bad as the legalistic minded people of Jesus' day? Or are we even worse?

Here is the last mention of Jesus teaching in a synagogue (v.10). The conflict between Jesus and legalistic religious leaders was intensifying. In the congregation was a crippled woman who was bent nearly double and she had been like that for eighteen years (v.11). As Jesus taught, he saw her and called her to come up to him (v.12). Those in the audience might not remember his words that day but they would never forget what he did. People remember what they see. This woman must have looked like her shoulders were tied almost to her knees. Jesus said to her, "You are released." With that he reached his hands to her and helped her to straighten up (v.13). For the first time in eighteen years she could look people squarely in the eye and she praised God.

When the director of the synagogue saw this, he was upset. It is interesting to note that he did not criticize Jesus. He may have feared him. Instead, in somewhat of a paternalistic manner, he scolded the people for coming on the sabbath to be healed (v.14). Jesus did not fear him and stopped him short with the charge that he was a hypocrite (v.15). The man wouldn't have hesitated to help a needy animal and here he was critical because a woman of long suffering was being helped. The opponents of Jesus were ashamed to say anything more. Everybody else was rejoicing over this wonderful thing Jesus had done.

Don't pass up an opportunity to do good or to rejoice over the good done by someone else.

KINGDOM REJECTS

Luke 13:18–35

What would it be like to come to the end of life, to wake up facing a closed door, and to hear a sentence of eternal condemnation? How does the kingdom of God grow and how does one come to be included in it?

Jesus compared the rule of God to two things. It was like a mustard seed that would grow into a tree size plant (v.19). This was a kind of mustard in that area and the illustration suggested a great increase from a small beginning. Many could hope to be included. The growth of the kingdom was like the fermentation process in bread dough (v.21). A little bit of leaven or fermented dough could cause a large mass of dough to become fermented. The chief process of the spread of God's kingdom has been through personal witness both to individuals and to crowds. An individual Christian is like a lump of leaven. He can share his faith with others.

As Jesus pressed on toward Jerusalem, a man asked him how many would be saved (v.23). Jesus did not answer his question but he advised his hearers to make a hard effort to get in (v.24). This isn't necessarily because it is difficult to get into the kingdom. But a complacent and unconcerned person may pass his opportunity by until it is too late (v.25). However, the entry is referred to as a narrow gate. A person can't just take everything and anything with him if he is going to live under the rule of God. Some who expect to gain personal privilege will not be admitted (v.28). On the other hand, people will be admitted into the kingdom who might be excluded from some earthly gatherings because of their geographical origin (v.29). Jesus then hinted rather ominously about impending desolation (v.35). Jerusalem was only a few years from facing destruction.

Your standing in the kingdom of God should be your greatest concern.

UNIT
7

The Worth of Persons

When someone asks how much another person is worth, he is nearly always inquiring about his financial status. Can the worth of a person be measured by his bank account? If so, then there are many worthless persons in the world.

Much has been said in modern times about the dignity of man and the worth of each individual. This concept is at the heart of political and social changes. Which should be valued the most, the individual human being or established customs and practices? The world has in it multitudes of needy, suffering people. But society acts as though they are not worth helping. You can tell what a person or society discounts and disapproves by the restrictive regulations developed.

Sometimes it seems that it is extremely difficult for the oppressed and the exploited people to get a hearing or even to get help. This situation is as old as the social groupings of men but in these days with our understanding of the dynamics of relationships and sociopolitical forces, we should be able to give attention to the helping of all kinds of individuals. This would magnify their worth.

Do individuals differ in worth or value? The answer to this question depends upon a person's life view. It might be said that a thing is worth whatever someone will pay for it. This could also be said about persons. A person's worth depends

75

upon somebody's love for him and the resources that the loving person can spend in his behalf. Jesus set the example for loving persons both by words and also by action. Chapters 14 and 15 of Luke are most helpful in seeing the worth that God attaches to individuals.

To Jesus a person was worth helping even in the face of going against social custom and tradition. It isn't position that gives a person value; it is really his responsiveness to the offered love of God. Responding to God calls for total commitment. A person should realize that he is thereby giving God his most precious possession, himself.

A person's greatest worth is his value to God. This is expressed in the three parables of Jesus about lost things. Man away from God is as worthless as a lost sheep, coin, or son. His worth is potential rather than practical. He is worth finding though. His worth is restored when he is found and in the presence of God.

Both immediately and ultimately a person's worth depends upon his relationships. Men judge the worth of another by his relation to things. This is immediate and temporary. Ultimately a person's worth is determined by his relation to God.

CONCERN FOR PERSONS

Luke 14:1–14

How much is a person worth? Nearly everyone has some system for ranking people. Some rank people according to their wealth. Some rank them according to their position. Some rank them according to their social prestige. How do you determine a person's worth?

Jesus was invited to a sabbath day dinner in a Pharisee's home (v.1). At the dinner, probably not as a guest but as an onlooker strolling in to the dining area of the open court, was a man with dropsy, a serious swelling or bloating of the body (v.2). Tension must have developed around the table as the diseased man came into the area. Jesus had not hesitated to heal on the sabbath before. Would he do so here, as a guest in the home of a strict Pharisee? Jesus did not seek to evade the problem. Before concentrating on the man himself, Jesus asked if it were legal to heal a person on the sabbath. The host and his other guests were silent (v.4). Jesus healed the man and let him go. But he wouldn't let go of the matter. He pressed the issue and asked if any of them would not rescue a work animal that might fall into a well on the sabbath (v.5). This kind of thing happened frequently. Very likely some at the table had rescued such an animal recently. Again they were silent. None of them wanted to say by implication that an animal was worth more than a man.

Ranking persons was serious with these people. A person sat at a table according to his rank. Jesus suggested that a person should start by ranking himself and that he should be modest about placing himself. It would be much better to be asked to move up rather than down (vv.9–10). Furthermore, Jesus instructed his hearers to be more generous in spreading their benefits (vv.12–13).

You can't lose by sharing with the needy. You will get it back and more at the resurrection (v.14).

GOD'S GUESTS

Luke 14:15–24

We are living in a time of plenty but people are starving. Some who are starving could live if they just had that which the affluent were throwing away. This reference is to physical food but doesn't it have its parallel and application in the spiritual area? Aren't there people who are rejecting opportunities that would be welcome to others?

As Jesus was eating at a dinner in a Pharisee's home, he spoke about judgment and the resurrection (see the Scripture passage before this). When one guest heard him mention the resurrection, he remarked that it would be wonderful to eat in the kingdom of God (v.15). This would be a logical remark for a pious person to make. He was looking forward to heaven. Jesus responded that he would be surprised at how many turn down the invitation of God.

In the parable Jesus described the kingdom of God as a banquet (v.16). In those days a man planning a banquet might invite friends in advance and at the time send a servant after them. When the dinner was ready, the invited guests made excuses and refused to attend. Three of the excuses were reported. One had bought land and needed to see it (v.18). Some are overly occupied with property and goods and lose sight of the promised land of the kingdom. Another said he had bought oxen and had to try them out (v.19). Work is one of the most important things in our culture but it should not distract one from kingdom service. A third excuse reported was that of the newly-wed (v.20). His excuse may have been the most socially polite in his day. But one should not let his loved ones separate him from God. With that the servant was sent out again and again to persuade people not ordinarily acceptable to become guests of his master (v.23).

God is willing to bless all people. Don't reject his goodness.

PAYING THE PRICE

Luke 14:25–35

Enthusiasm that is not counterbalanced by realism may lead to humiliation. Have you counted the cost of following Christ in your situation? Are you willing to pay that price?

The indifference of the spiritual leaders to Jesus in the previous passage is a contrast to the wild acclaim of the multitudes here (v.25). Jesus cautioned them that following him could have serious consequences. A person couldn't follow Jesus with mental reservations. He had to be willing to leave everything, even his dearest loved ones. His supreme loyalty to Jesus would make his action toward his family seem like hate (v.26). The person who would become a disciple must do it with no turning back (v.27).

Some would ask, "Doesn't it pay to serve Jesus?" Yes, it does. But it also costs. Sometimes we press people so much to accept Christ that we do them the disservice of not challenging them to be willing to pay the price. If we started out to build a tower, wouldn't we wisely estimate the cost (v.28)? An unfinished building is a monument to shortsightedness. A Christian should take the long look and commit himself fully to Christ. This would call for a person to lay a good foundation for Christian usefulness and to develop his life strongly phase by phase. Another illustration used by Jesus was that of a king about to go to war with another king (v.31). He should know his enemy, consider his own strength, and plan the proper course of action. The point Jesus was making was for the need of complete, purposeful commitment to him.

One's commitment to Christ should be like good salt. Its quality should be the highest. Anything less is worthless (vv.34–35).

A word to the wise should be adequate. You have noted what Jesus said; then do it.

WORTH FINDING

Luke 15:1–10

What do you think God is like? Do you understand he cares for the individual person and will take the initiative in reaching him?

People like Luke 15. They can see themselves in it.

Social polarization was rigid in Jesus' day but he paid no attention to it. When Pharisees who felt they were superior to others criticized him (v.2), Jesus answered with three parables. Look at the first two together.

Any shepherd who lost a sheep would go out looking for it (v.4). How far would he go to find it? What is God's limit in his search for straying mankind? The limit of God is his love. He would die for you to save you. The words of Jesus were a rebuke to his critics. They had more compassion for animals than for men. They could understand a shepherd risking his life for a lost sheep and rejoicing over its recovery (v.6). But they couldn't see much worth in a person reduced to the state of an animal by poverty and ignorance. Jesus shocked them by saying that God and all heaven rejoices over a sinner's conversion (v.7). The opponents of Jesus identified themselves with the ninety-nine who needed no repentence. They were sullen about God's joy over the salvation of sinners.

Jesus had something more to say. Any woman who lost money equivalent to a day's pay would hunt it frantically until she found it (v.8). Some have emphasized the small worth of a single coin but it was a day's wage in those times. Her house was probably a small dark hut with a hard dirt floor covered with cuttings of grass and weeds as a kind of cushion. Can you imagine hunting a coin in that? But she found it and called people to rejoice with her (v.2). God is like that in finding lost persons (v.10).

God feels you are worth finding. Are you?

THE LOVING FATHER

Luke 15:11–24

Ask again, What is God like? Do you understand he is like a loving father? Look carefully at the father in this parable of the prodigal son.

The father was forsaken. The younger son asked for his inheritance ahead of time (v.12). He left then to go into a country far from his father. One life-style was rejected for another. The young man felt he could find his own fulfilment only by breaking with the past. He was willing to use his father's accumulated wealth in his defiance.

The father waited and watched. He could envision his son squandering the money in extravagance (v.13). He knew the ruin that would follow. When hope was gone, the son resorted to the worst occupation a Jew could imagine (v.15). When a life starts down, its degradation may be unlimited. God is like a loving father waiting hopefully for a wandering son to come home. Here this parable differs from the first two. A son is not like a sheep or a coin. He has the potential of coming to his senses (v.17). A person in sin is not normal; he is not at himself. He would be better off as a slave of God than as a rebel against him. What a cleansing of the soul when one can face himself honestly! The thing to do is to go home and ask forgiveness.

The father forgave. As he watched, he recognized his returning son at a great distance (v.20). The son's confession was interrupted by his father's outburst of love. He called for his son to be invested with the benefits of sonship—a robe, a ring, and shoes. Love can know the greatest hurt and love can know the greatest joy. No joy can compare to that of a loving father with his lost son in his arms. That is a time for feasting (v.24).

Do you realize how much God loves you as an individual person? To understand that is to come to one's senses.

UNBROTHERLINESS

Luke 15:25–32

What credentials must a person have to be accepted by Christians? That is a more serious question than some may think. Jesus was accepting people whom the religious leaders of his day could not tolerate.

The parable of the prodigal son does not end with the father's order for the feast. The faithful, older son who had been working in the field returned to find the feast in progress (v.25). A servant told him that his brother had come home and his father was giving him a feast with a full orchestra and entertainment (v.27). The older son was angry and sulked outside (v.28). The father came out to him and pleaded with him to be understanding. He flung his hurt in the face of his father and revealed years of resentment and ill-will that had built up inside him (v.29). He cited his own faithfulness and lack of recognition (v.29). This seemed to him to be the climax in a series of wrongs. His indignation had been mounting until it was an unreasoning fury. He indicted his father along with his brother by referring to the prodigal as "that son of yours" (v.30). It was as though he accused his father of condoning the sins of the wayward son. He probably would have felt better if the sinner had been severely reprimanded and put on probation if not even rejected.

The father patiently reminded him that his inheritance was still intact. All the father had left belonged to the older son and it would be honored (v.31). Then he justified his action by saying it was proper to rejoice because the dead was alive, the lost was found. As a further appeal, he referred to the prodigal as "your brother" (v.32).

The story doesn't really end. Its conclusion is left to the hearer. What kind of an ending will you write to this parable? You will write it with your life.

UNIT
8

Life's Ends

A person needs to know where he is going or he may not know he is there when he arrives. To a great extent the purpose of life has been a major concern so far in these comments of Luke. Now, though, as we move in closer to the time of the death of Jesus, let us concentrate further on life objectives as we look at chapters 16, 17, and 18 of Luke. Having clear understanding of what he wants to accomplish will help a person in several ways. Such goals will be guidelines to him in making choices or decisions. On what basis might a person select one alternative over another? Unless he knows where he wants to go, he may resort to expediency or immediate sensation as the ground for choice. A second value in having life goals is that they may help a person evaluate his course and correct it if need be. How can a person assess his actions if he doesn't know the results he wants?

One can hardly set life objectives without considering what place material goods will play. One must decide whether he is going to become a slave of money or make all that he has instrumental to his goals. The matter is really deeper than that. The choice is whether a person will be a slave of material gain or a steward of God. This means that one must analyze his set of values. What will he worship? Or, asking the same question in different words, what will he count to be of the greatest worth? That is what he will "worth-ship." The parable of the rich man and Lazarus will be helpful in thinking about this.

Life is not like a writer's first draft that can be rewritten and improved over and over. As you live your life, every day and every act is a final draft. There can be no re-doing or deletions. We can be forgiven for our sins but the consequences of them may continue in humanity's course until the end of time. Therefore we should think carefully what we want to be like as Christians. We need to live in constant awareness of the goodness of God and be praising him for it. Furthermore we ought to be realistic about the coming of the end. It's certain. Luke 17 will help in thinking about the finality of life.

A human problem is that of fixation on wrong objectives. One must be willing to test continually all that he holds to. This doesn't mean to live in a state of agnosticism or doubt. It does mean that one ought to avoid conceit and pride. He should not be too proud to ask God for help. Nor should he be so conceited that he does not realize his need for God's help. Objectives can be a hindrance instead of a help if they become restrictive limitations to the fulfilment of a person's life. How can this be prevented? One needs to maintain an openness to God. This kind of disposition is illustrated in the praying of the tax collector, the simple trust of children, and the cry of the blind beggar.

A person should have objectives in life. Furthermore, he needs a continual awareness of the presence of God in his life and to be responsive to God's leadership. In this manner he can move toward his objectives with confidence and courage.

THE WAY TO USE MONEY

Luke 16:1–13

Some think their problems could be solved if they just had money. It's hard for them to realize that having money creates a problem. If you had money, what would you do with it? That question isn't meant to be funny. What would you do if a large sum came to you suddenly? How do you use the money you now have? Do you use it wisely?

Jesus told of a clever rogue that may have been the talk of the country at that time (v.1). This was an agent whose mismanagement had been discovered. He was instructed to bring his books in for an accounting or audit (v.2). The man was dishonest but he probably had not involved others up to this point. Now, though, he went to the debtors, discounting their bills in order to obligate them to him (vv.4–7). His employer praised him for his shrewdness. Jesus did not condone any of the evil actions. He made four comments that seemed related to this story.

He indicated that wicked people often plan better than Christians (v.8). What great good could churches do if they planned as carefully as bank robbers?

Jesus advised his disciples that money was worth the most as it related to the future and especially to the everlasting habitations (v.9).

Then he pointed out that honesty is a way of life. A person trustworthy in minor matters can be trusted with major concerns (v.10). One's use of money may reveal his true character.

Jesus spoke further about the impossibility of divided loyalty. In those days a slave could not possibly serve two masters (v.13). This was an illustration of the choice one must make. A person cannot possibly serve God and any other master, even money.

What is your choice?

ETERNAL RICHES

Luke 16:14–31

What will be the end of the life committed to concerns of this world? Values may be reversed in heaven.

Jesus had said that a person couldn't serve both God and money. The Pharisees sneered at this because they considered prosperity to be a mark of divine favor (v.14). Jesus responded by suggesting that men and God do not always put the same value on things (v.15).

Some things do last. Among them are God's criteria or his laws (v.17). An example of this is the value that God places on the home (v.18). The relation of husband and wife had deteriorated in Jesus' day until it was as bad or even worse than today's situation.

Jesus told a story heavy with irony. It had in it two chief characters. One was nameless. How strange—in view of the fact that he was rich, clothed in the costliest garb, and dining daily in luxury (v.19). A person like that is never nameless in modern-day journalism. The other man was Lazarus. He was a poverty case, ill, eating garbage, and unable to kick away the dogs licking his running sores (vv.20–21). He died, which was no surprise, but surprisingly he was carried by angels directly to heaven (v.22). The rich man also died. Affluence can be as hard on a human being as poverty. His destination in death was torment. He could see Lazarus in Abraham's bosom in heaven (v.23). He had not given mercy to Lazarus but he asked that Lazarus be sent to him in mercy (v.24). The values he accepted on earth were reversed in heaven (v.25). However, the gulf he had established between himself and Lazarus was fixed for eternity (v.26). He asked that at least his brothers be warned. God had already given them warning in Moses and the prophets (v.31). One rejecting the Scriptures would not believe a resurrected person.

Look past this life and see what is really valuable.

WHAT A CHRISTIAN IS LIKE

Luke 17:1–10

It is wonderful to be a good Christian but it isn't easy. There are things a Christian shouldn't do and other things he should do.

A Christian should not cause someone to do wrong. People are certain to be tempted but it would be better to die than to cause even the least persons to sin (v.2). This presses further the responsibility that Cain refused to recognize (Gen. 4:9) when he responded to God, "Am I my brother's keeper?"

Reverse the situation. What if someone offends a Christian? Why, get it out in the open, and if the person repents, forgive him. That would be hard but it would be good. How forgiving should the disciple be? He should be willing to keep on forgiving, even seven times a day (v.4). That is more than any other religion asks.

A lot is expected of a Christian. The apostles asked for more faith (v.5). Jesus' answer implied that they didn't have much. If they had a tiny bit of real faith, they could have called upon the unlimited power of God (v.6). If someone can't forgive because he has something in his heart against another, he can ask with a tiny bit of faith and God will help him get rid of his prejudice and forgive.

There is the temptation for a Christian to be proud of doing what he ought to do. This would be like a slave doing what he was supposed to do and then expecting his master to wait on him (v.7). A follower of Christ is expected to work, but in doing it, he doesn't put God in debt to him. Christians cannot build up enough credit to be superior to God. They should recognize that they haven't done any big thing when they have just done their duty (v.10).

God's goodness is based upon his mercy and not upon our merit. Think about it and thank him.

THE BEAUTY OF GRATITUDE

Luke 17:11–19

How good it is to be appreciated! Persons have wept in joy because someone thought to speak words of gratitude.

As Jesus traveled to Jerusalem he came to a village between Galilee and Samaria. He met a large group of lepers composed evidently of both Galilean Jews and Samaritans (v.12). Ordinarily they would have had nothing to do with one another but suffering puts people on common ground. They stopped a good distance from Jesus as they were supposed to do. Lepers were outcasts and were not permitted to approach other people. Therefore, they sometimes found community in banding together. In loud voices they called to Jesus for mercy (v.13). A person who recovered from leprosy was to go to the priests for confirmation of his good health and for permission to re-enter society. When these lepers asked Jesus for help, he told them to go show themselves to the priests (v.14). They acted in faith and started for the priests and they were healed.

When one of them saw that he was healed, he whirled around and ran toward Jesus praising God at the top of his voice (v.15). He threw himself at the feet of Jesus, thanking him (v.16). His speech revealed that he was a Samaritan. Jesus was pleased with this man's action and he raised the question about the other nine (v.17). Why didn't they return to Jesus also? That is a good question. Why don't people act more like they are thankful to God for his mercy? Jesus even suggested that this man's gratitude was less expected than that of the others since he was a stranger (v.18). Then he spoke to the man directly. He commanded him to stand up and to go his way. He had made a commitment of life that affected his whole being (v.19).

If the silence of the majority is ingratitude, then let's join the minority expressing its appreciation to God.

THE TIME OF THE END

Luke 17:20–37

Have you wondered when the end will be? Many have wondered about this. The question is difficult to answer. It depends on what you mean by it.

The Pharisees evidently had in mind a question like this when they asked Jesus when the kingdom of God was coming (v.20). Jesus did not answer the question. It was as though the question itself were not valid. Would it be proper to ask when is God going to take over the rule of the world? Jesus advised the Pharisees they would not be alerted to the coming of the kingdom by prearranged warning signals. It was not to be discovered by external searching but to be realized by an internal, personal experience (v.21). God increases his rule of the world as individuals obey him.

Jesus knew his disciples would also have questions about the future. He told them that the time would come when Christians would long to see the Son of man (v.22). People should not be deceived by some telling them that the Christ had returned (v.23). The appearance of the Son of man would be as clear and unmistakable as lightning (v.24). Jesus wanted his disciples to understand, though, that the immediate future held suffering for him—and, by implication, for them (v.25). As far as his being revealed in the future, this would be as sudden and unexpected as the flood or the destruction of Sodom (vv.26–29). People would be going about the ordinary concerns of life. The advice for that time is not to be too concerned about material things nor too attached to the past (vv.31–32). A person could be lost by having too great concern for his life (v.33). The important thing then will not be your work or your associates but what are you (vv.34–35).

The question was still where and when. Jesus said it would be at the appropriate time like the gathering of birds of prey (v.37). The real question is, "Are you ready?"

PRAYING WITH PURPOSE

Luke 18:1–14

One's understanding of the end or purpose of life affects his praying. Do you persist in prayer? Do you pray properly?

Jesus advised his disciples to pray continually and not to become discouraged (v.1). With that he told them a parable that taught the importance of persistent praying. It started with a judge who was both irreligious and unsympathetic (v.2). A widow asked him for an injunction against someone who was causing her trouble (v.3). This may have been a debtor not paying her what he owed or a creditor making an unjust demand. The widow evidently had no money to offer the judge nor influence to exert on him. He would not hear her at first but because of her persistence he responded to her plea. Jesus recognized that this judge was unjust and then he contrasted him to God. If an unjust judge will respond favorably to a persistent petitioner, might we not count on God to answer his own people who pray earnestly (v.7)? God is faithful. But, when the Son of man comes, will he find people being faithful (v.8)?

Next Jesus drew a caricature in words. Among his hearers were some self-righteous persons who had no use for others (v. 9). He described two men going to pray who were quite different. One was a Pharisee who reported to God how satisfied he was with himself (vv.11–12). He had no request to make of God because he couldn't think of anything that God had that he wanted. Prayer that is made because it is proper isn't proper prayer.

The other man was a tax collector. His society despised him but he despised himself even more. His only hope was that perhaps God wouldn't despise him. He begged God for mercy and he went home forgiven and satisfied (v.14).

Don't waste prayer with self-applause. Be realistic and ask God for his loving help.

SIMPLE TRUST AND SOPHISTICATED DISBELIEF

Luke 18:15–30

What is easy for a child and difficult for an adult? The answer could be "to give up everything in order to trust Christ completely." Two incidents in Luke illustrate this.

People brought their little children to Jesus for him to bless (v.15). This was not an unusual request to make of outstanding teachers. The disciples were overly protective and sought to guard Jesus from these well-meaning parents. He corrected them and told them not to prevent children from coming to him. Little children can respond easily to the idea of God's rule. Their kind of response is what everyone must have even to enter the kingdom (v.17). This would amount to an openness to learn and to trust, a readiness to love and to obey, and a desire to please and to help.

The other incident described by Luke is a contrast. A Jewish ruler asked Jesus how he could inherit eternal life. His question seemed to indicate he was interested in only the minimum requirements (v.18). Jesus quoted five of the commandments that referred to his relations with other people (v.20). Without reflecting on what Jesus told him, he responded that he was perfect in all of his dealings with others (v.21). He may have lived a well-ordered life but the omission of love from it was obvious. Jesus advised him to take drastic action: sell all he had, give it to the poor, and follow him (v.21). Why did Christ demand so much of this man? He did it because the man had so much to give. He didn't ask of him a thing that he didn't have to give. The man had hoarded goods needed by others to live and felt no guilt. Jesus gave him the grand opportunity to make up for it all in one action. The man might have had the potential to become the chief disciple of Jesus. But he turned away sadly.

Remember, no one ever really gives up anything for Christ. He receives so much from Christ both now and hereafter!

CLOSED MINDS AND OPENED EYES

Luke 18:31–43

Death is closer today than it was yesterday. Are there things you need to see to? Are there words you need to say to others? Are there kind acts you need to do? Jesus had a date with death. The place was Jerusalem and he was on his way there with his disciples.

Jesus needed to help the twelve understand what was awaiting them at their destination (v.31). The words of the prophets would be fulfilled but the disciples had not fully accepted the prophecies that pointed to the suffering of the Messiah. Jesus told them clearly that he would be mocked, scourged, and killed and that he would then rise on the third day (vv.32–33). It was almost as though the disciples did not even hear him. They had their minds made up and they were only hearing what they wanted to hear.

On his way to Jerusalem Jesus came to Jericho. A blind man at the side of the road heard the commotion made by the crowd collecting around Jesus (v.36). Upon inquiring, he was told that Jesus of Nazareth was passing by. He had heard enough about him to know who he was. He even believed that Jesus was the Messiah and so indicated it by calling him "Son of David" (v.38). He called out to Jesus for mercy. People around him heartlessly rebuked him and sought to silence him. But he cried again at the top of his voice. Jesus heard him and stopped. When the man was brought to him, he made the man say what he wanted (v.41). God has blessings that may be enjoyed only by those who earnestly desire them. Note what the man did when he had his sight. He followed Jesus, praising God (v.43).

Review the contrast in these two incidents. Do not be a disciple with a closed mind. Instead of that, magnify the lordship of Christ and follow him, praising God for the salvation he has given you.

UNIT
9

Challenged by Controversy

In a day of massive, accelerated communication controversy is almost inevitable. If people who have different backgrounds are involved in sharing ideas, their differences will begin to be expressed. Then people will group together as they find others with views similar to theirs. This is polarization. Where differences of views are contradictory and people become threatened by the ideas of others, controversy will develop.

How can we understand controversy around us and in which we might be involved? How should we meet it and how should we react to those who attack our basic convictions? Chapters 18, 19, and 20 in Luke can help us develop some guidelines and approaches for confrontations we may have with others.

The last several days before the crucifixion were days of intensive controversy for Jesus. It seems that as he approached Jerusalem the tension and conflict around him increased. For instance in Jericho the crowd almost turned against him as he gave attention to the man Zaccheus. There before he faced the last clash with his opponents in Jerusalem, he reasserted his mission which was to seek and save the lost. One must be careful that controversy does not divert him from his life purpose. Fear of one's own inability may be as ruinous as concern about the criticism of enemies. A parable of Jesus reminded his hearers of their accountability.

A person should not only know where he stands but he should also act in accordance with that stance. Jesus did this as he rode triumphantly into Jerusalem. No one doubted then that he was acting like the Messiah. This act of the Lord precipitated an alliance of forces that had not before been able to join together. One may have to invite controversy in order to accomplish his purpose. Jesus could look ahead and see the consequences of his actions. Jerusalem's rejection of him would seal her doom and Jesus wept because of this. He also saw that in cleansing the Temple he would trigger the chain of events that would climax in a few days with his death.

A person needs to be sure of himself as he faces controversy. He must be sure of his authority. This was the first point of attack that Jesus' enemies made on him. He threw the issue back to them in such a way that they avoided discussing it further. But Jesus discussed it further in a parable to the people in which he revealed to them the significance of the conflict going on in their presence. The ultimate authority, of course, is more than political; it is religious. Caesar's demands must be met but even more so must God's demands be met.

At the root of controversy is the conflict of ideas or concepts. This was illustrated in the response of Jesus to a question that challenged the credibility of resurrection. The problem was that some highly intelligent men didn't understand what they were talking about. Then Jesus spoke words which, if properly understood, could change one's concepts of heaven, of the Christ, and even of oneself.

We can be grateful for the controversy that Jesus faced. The answers he gave in these trying situations are some of the greatest help we have in the complex problems of our modern day.

SAVING THE UNWORTHY

Luke 19:1–10

Some people had a hard time understanding Jesus. He was unconcerned about class distinction. Also he would turn from a crowd to help an individual sincerely seeking him.

Jesus was in Jericho, one of the richest cities of that part of the world. It was an intersection of commercial routes in a fertile agricultural valley. The tax office in it was the most important and lucrative of the area. The director of this revenue office was Zaccheus (v.2). He was a Jew who had gained rank and riches at the price of rejection by his countrymen. Life was lonely for him. He heard of Jesus' presence in the city and was motivated to seek him. He was not a large man and the growing crowd around Jesus shoved him farther away rather than helping him (v.3). But he looked ahead of the procession and saw a tree to which he ran and climbed. When Jesus came to the tree, he looked up and saw him (v.5) The climax of a person's search for Christ is to realize that Christ has been searching for him. Jesus called Zaccheus down from the tree in order that he might go home with him. This was a courageous act on the part of Jesus because he was immediately criticized for associating with such a man, a sinner (19:7). Zaccheus wanted to make a change. He had not become what he had hoped to be. He had gained position and possessions but he didn't like himself any better than the crowd liked him. With the help of Christ's presence he reversed his life pattern. He promised half of his property to the poverty stricken and to pay back four times anything he had cheated people out of. Jesus approved this. A man was saved and his deeds demonstrated it. The threatening controversy was quieted by Jesus' statement that he came to seek the lost and save them (v.10).

I wouldn't argue about whom the Lord should save, would you?

COURAGE VERSUS CAUTION

Luke 19:11–27

Jesus spoke rather sternly to the crowd as they approached Jerusalem. Excitement was mounting as some talked about an immediate appearance of the kingdom of God (v.11).

Jesus told a story that paralleled a bit of recent history. In somewhat the same way that Archelaus had gone to Rome to have his inherited kingship confirmed, the leading character went to a far country for a similar purpose (v.12). Giving ten of his servants equal sums of money he told them to use the amounts till he returned (v.13). They were free to do entirely as they pleased with only the stipulation that they would eventually report on their actions. The man had enemies who sought to keep him from becoming king. He received his kingdom, though, and returned. He called first for his servants. The story included the reports of three of them.

One had increased the amount trusted to him ten times. This was the kind of man the king wanted to depend on and he promoted him to be governor of ten cities (v.17). Persons of great authority must have people under them who are trustworthy.

The second servant had increased his money five times and the king had work for him—the rule of five cities (v.19).

Then came the servant who was not risk-oriented. He had been afraid of failure. He was weakened by his resentment toward responsibility. He wrapped the money up in a cloth he should have used to wipe his sweating face (v.20). The king reprimanded him and relieved him of what he had. The man who did the most could handle a little more and so he gave it to him (v.24). One bit of unfinished business was the execution of his opponents. In this last statement Jesus may have warned of the coming destruction of Jerusalem.

Great achievement calls for great risk. Are you willing to attempt great things for God?

DIVINE PROTOCOL

Luke 19:28–40

How should Christ be properly presented? He made his own choice on how he should enter Jerusalem at this time so soon before his death.

Jesus was walking ahead of the crowd when he approached two villages near the Mount of Olives (v.29). There he paused and waited for two of his disciples to go after a colt in a nearby village. The availability of this colt was evidently by prearrangement. If they were questioned, they would be able to take the colt simply by saying, "The Lord needs it" (v.34). Things happened as Jesus had predicted and they returned with a colt that had not yet been ridden by anyone. It was a donkey colt. This was not as inappropriate as we might think. Solomon rode a mule in his royal procession. Courtly etiquette called for a king to ride a horse to war but a mule or donkey in peace. By entering Jerusalem on a colt Jesus intentionally fulfilled a messianic sign people had been looking for (Zech. 9:9).

No one could doubt that Jesus was offering himself as the Messiah of prophecy. The charge of excitement increased in the crowd accompanying Christ now riding on the colt. They were spreading their cloaks along the road as a carpet. Then as they crested the Mount of Olives, all constraint was gone. A thunder of shouted praise reverberated down the slopes. Luke recorded the phrases that would communicate most to his Gentile readers. The Pharisees were alarmed. This incident could inflame Jerusalem to the point of revolution and extensive bloodshed before the week was over. They cautioned Jesus and advised him to restrain his disciples (v.39). They were saying this was his responsibility.

Be warned, though. If men resort to stony silence, stones themselves will be given voices with which to praise God (v.40). Praise him! Praise him!

CONFLICTING EMOTIONS

Luke 19:41–48

How much emotion did Jesus experience? We find him at times undergoing strong feelings.

He and the crowd advanced toward Jerusalem for the triumphal entry. At a place on the Mount of Olives they could see the city. Jesus wept over it like a bereaved person at a funeral (v.41). He could foresee that Jerusalem was on a collision course with catastrophe. The messianic commitment of Jewish leaders was to a military and political victory over Rome. The inevitable confrontation would result in destruction. Jesus could see the coming siege, the slaughter, and the devastation (vv.43–44). Jerusalem's only hope was to turn from blind nationalism to accept the Messiah who that day was riding into the city on a donkey colt. But they couldn't understand this was God coming to them.

Jesus went on to the Temple where money changers and sellers of sacrificial animals profaned the place. He drove them out charging that by their exploitation of religion they had perverted the house of prayer (v.46). Jesus had attacked a profitable business venture owned by the high priest family and Temple authorities. By thus defying the power structure he had signed his own death warrant.

The next several days were like a grim game of stalking the prey. Jesus continued daily facing those who were seeking to kill him. The tension increased as he taught. A marvelous learning situation had developed. People hung upon his words (v.47). A coalition was formed of the religious leaders and the persons who had influence with the people. Plotting and scheming was taking place to destroy him but he came freely to the Temple and talked boldly to the people.

In general we are inclined to avoid controversy. We must have the courage, though, to face conflict if it comes from telling people about Christ.

ARGUMENT OVER AUTHORITY

Luke 20:1–8

When a person begins to disturb established order, he can expect to be challenged at the point of authority.

The opponents of Jesus had agreed on his death and sought to trap him into making an indiscreet statement to justify their action. If possible they had to discredit him in the eyes of the people and also to legitimize his execution.

This was a day full of challenges and attack. It began with an impressive deputation from the Sanhedrin. The group was composed of top officials of the Temple, legal authorities, and prominent Jewish leaders (v.1). Jesus had acted with great authority. He had entered Jerusalem as the Messiah and had cleansed the Temple. What he had done was either proper or presumptious. The committee asked him what authority he had and who gave it to him (v.2). This was a logical question and it was a good opening move for the day.

Jesus was looked on as a rabbi and he acted like one. He responded to a question by asking one. The question was on authority and so he turned his attention back to the beginning of his ministry and asked if the baptism of John was from heaven or of men (20:4). This was the perfect counter move. Jesus forced his inquisitors to reconsider their own question. The answer to the second question would also answer the first.

Jesus' question had only two possible answers but his opponents saw their dilemma. To answer one way would mean they would have to accept John and also Jesus. To answer the other way would be to arouse the wrath of the people and to risk death at the hands of a mob (vv.5–6). They chose to retreat and to suffer damage to their status. When they claimed ignorance and refused to express an opinion, Jesus properly refused to answer their question.

Recognize your responsibility to God and his authority over you.

THE VINDICATION OF AUTHORITY

Luke 20:9–18

Authority that is absolute will ultimately triumph. We have no cause to fear anything. God will be victorious.

After Jesus had answered the challenge to his authority, he turned to the people and told them a parable. In a way he appealed to the court of public opinion. Perhaps he hoped that the people would understand enough of the significance of what was going on that they would not be swept along in the rebellion of their leaders against God.

The meaning of the parable was clear. The man represented God. The vineyard he planted represented Israel. The husbandmen or tenants represented the leaders (v.10). The messengers or servants represented the prophets (vv.10–12). Each servant was treated worse than the one before him. Israel's leaders had acted as though they would never have to give an account to God. Then in the parable the man decided to send his beloved son (v.13). The son obviously represented Jesus and the people evidently understood this. Then Jesus told them of the son's murder (v.15). There can be no doubt from this that Jesus knew that his death was imminent. He may even have been goading his enemies into action. The parable concluded with the return of the owner and his destruction of the faithless tenants (v.16). The hearers responded impulsively, "God forbid!" They were horrified.

Jesus gripped them with his eyes and quoted to them Psalm 118:22. The report was that in the building of the Temple the stonemasons had laid aside an odd-shaped piece only to discover that it was designed to be the cornerstone (v.17). This became a favorite reference of early Christians. Jesus alluded to two other passages about stones—a stone upon which one might stumble and be broken (Isa. 8:14) or one which might fall on one and crush him (Dan. 2:34,44).

Wait and see! God will triumph.

100

GOD OR CAESAR

Luke 20:19–26

When it comes to authority, how do you draw the line between civil authority and religious authority? Which is superior? Jesus was asked a question something like that.

The opponents of Jesus were so angry after he told the parable about the faithless vineyard keepers that they wanted to seize him immediately. However, they were afraid of the people (v.19).

They became more determined in their conspiring to trap him in an injudicious statement. They decided to seek to lead him to comment on the political situation that he might be charged with inciting people to insurrection (v.20). Spies sought to disarm him with flattery. They praised him for being forthright and speaking without fear and with respect only for God. Watch out when men praise you too carefully. Then they punched at him the question of the rightness of Roman taxation (v.22).

Jesus saw through their trickery. At his request a coin was handed to him. He asked whose image and name was on it (v.24). A ruler of a land minted the coinage and claimed it as his own possession. On this ground he could legally assess taxation. When Jesus was told Caesar's image and name were on the coin, he told them to give Caesar that which belonged to Caesar. But he said more. He told them also to give God what belongs to God (v.25). What belongs to God? Well, what is marked with his image? Man may owe taxes to his government but he owes himself to God. This will qualify his every other obligation. The Christian should be a better citizen than anyone else. Yet he must be willing to die if need be to deliver his testimony for Christ to others. The agents of his enemies could say nothing more (v.26).

Is there a commitment that you need to rethink? Have you fully given to God those things that are his?

RESURRECTION: HOPE OR DREAM

Luke 20:27–40

Is resurrection a valid hope for reasonable people? Or, is it the absurd fantasy of wishful thinking?

The Sadducees probably looked on themselves as realistic people. They were a religiopolitical group that held strictly to the writings of Moses. They claimed they could find nothing there about resurrection (v.27). Nor did they believe in angels, spirits, or a divine plan for an individual life. The Sadducees controlled the Temple. Being rich, they favored keeping the status quo and opposed any disturbance.

Others had failed to trap Jesus with questions and so the Sadducees decided to ask him one they had used often with success. To begin with, they identified their authority which was Moses (Deut. 25:5–6). This was like beginning with a premise no one could reject. On this they constructed an absurd hypothetical situation: a woman marrying and becoming widowed to seven brothers in turn (vv.28–31). Hoping to ridicule Jesus, the Sadducees asked him whose wife the woman would be in the resurrection (v.33). With smug contempt they awaited his answer thinking he would either have to oppose the authority of Moses or say something that would make him a laughingstock.

First Jesus advised them their concept of heaven was not valid. Functions are different in this life and the life to come. Relationships also are different and have other purposes than procreation (v.35). Then Jesus confirmed resurrection. He presented an argument no one had thought of. Moses had called the Lord the God of Abraham, Isaac, and Jacob. He argued that these men were alive or the Lord could not have been called their God. An amazed murmur went through the crowd and several legal experts commended him for his answer. That ended their questioning of him.

Thank God anew for your hope of resurrection.

CONCEPTS THAT NEED CHANGING

Luke 20:41–47

People are inclined to hold tenaciously to ideas or concepts. Changes in behavior and action are not apt to come until certain concepts are changed.

The opponents of Jesus were determined to do away with him. This was basically because of their concept of the Messiah. They had understood Jesus' claim to be the Messiah but he wasn't the kind of promised deliverer that fitted their concept. They had looked for a military-political leader who would bring the Jewish people back to the greatness they had known under David and Solomon. They were fond of referring to the Messiah as the son of David. Jesus had answered their questions and evaded every trap they had set for him. Now he asked them a question not to embarrass them or to trap them but to show them the error in their messianic idea. Referring to a passage in Psalm 110:1, Jesus asked how the Messiah could be thought of as David's son when David called him Lord (v.44). No one was able to answer him. Jesus was saying that the Messiah would be more than a son of David. It was evident to them that he was human; he was also affirming to them that he was divine.

Their inadequate concept of Christ was accentuated by their inflated concept of themselves. Jesus spoke to all of the people around warning them of these scholars of the law (v.45). They expected honor and loved preferential treatment. Such an element is not good for a society. Many trusting people, such even as needy widows, can be duped out of their life necessities by these vain posers of piety (v.47). Jesus spoke harshly against persons who exploited religion for personal gain. As Jesus faced those who were seeking to kill him, he did not flinch from indicting them for their crimes against humanity and God.

Test all of your ideas with the teachings of Christ.

103

The Bitter Cup

Tragedy has struck again and again in our day. On television we have witnessed assassinations and seen the victims of floods, earthquakes, and wars. Sometimes we have wept but we have learned to forget quickly. Also there are those who have experienced personal tragedy, whose arms ache for loved ones who will never return. Life has burdens of heartache and trouble that make time creep in slow agony. Sometimes one must undergo an experience that he shrinks from with the strongest desire to escape. Life can become a bitter cup to drink.

With an excessive exposure through the news media to calamities in our day we may become insensitive to the needs of people. No trouble comes that God is not aware of or unconcerned about. Jesus foresaw the destruction of Jerusalem and warned people of its coming. These words of warning of the disaster were a kind of prelude to the events immediately ahead for Jesus personally.

One tragedy for Jesus was the failure of a disciple of his. Judas betrayed him. Many people will have the experience of a friend turning against them. This is a hard thing to take and the best source of comfort is Christ himself. No one has suffered more than he has from a betrayal.

When a person sees a storm coming, he needs to prepare for

it to the best of his ability. Jesus sought to help his followers become ready for the crisis they would face. He did this through personal guidance imparting to them courage by his own example. Furthermore, he led them in an experience which they could repeat through the years as a reminder of what he had done for them. This was the Lord's Supper. In addition then he carefully instructed them regarding their attitude and actions for the days ahead.

Do we dare anticipate what the worst could be? Jesus faced it and resorted to prayer. He asked for relief but received strength. The only door open to him led to a cross. He had to face his enemies alone and to die deserted and forsaken. There was no escape for him. He was able to protect his disciples at the time of his arrest and to make certain that they were released unharmed. He rejoiced over their deliverance. However, he was saddened as Peter tried to stay close to him but out of fear for his own life denied knowing him. Subjected to indignities and insults, he was finally indicted for blasphemy. How ironic and bitter that the Son of God should be tried for saying he was the Christ!

If we were to stop at this point in the life of Christ, it might seem proper to judge that he was defeated. But read carefully chapters 21 and 22 of Luke. Christ agreed to drink a bitter cup but he was not defeated.

COST OR VALUE

Luke 21:1–4

There is a difference between the cost of things and their value. A dollar would have different value to different people. In one situation it might not even pay the tip for a dinner but in another it might provide the whole dinner for a hungry family. The use of money affects its value. So does one's attitude toward it and the amount of it that a person has.

These four verses fit well with the preceding chapter of Luke. Just before this Jesus had warned the people about the vanity of the scribes, the legal experts. He was sitting in the Temple area where people brought their money gifts. This was the treasury with receptacles shaped like trumpets or megaphones. Jesus looked up and saw the wealthy making a show of their giving (v.1). He was not pleased. Making a display of religion is in the same class as using religion for personal gain. As he watched, a widow came to make her offering seeking to be inconspicuous. She gave the least amount one could give and have the offering accepted. This amounted to two thin copper coins (v.2)

Jesus commented on the woman's gift. He rated it higher than all the others (v.3). Others had given without any loss to themselves. Their apparently large gifts were only a small percentage of the total of their possessions. A gift that a person can afford to give cannot be called a sacrifice. But the woman lived in poverty. When she gave the minimum amount that a person could give, she gave her maximum. She gave all she had and withheld nothing. She needed what she gave. This was total commitment. The gift was of great value because of the spirit of the giver and because it was a sacrifice she could not afford.

How would Christ evaluate our gifts to him?

SERIOUS TROUBLE AHEAD

Luke 21:5–24

If trouble is coming, does it help to know it?

As Jesus left the Temple, someone commented on the massive marble stones (v.5). The Temple, built by Herod the Great, was magnificent and looked like it would stand forever. Jesus said, though, that not even one stone of it would be left on another (v.6). The Romans reduced it to rubble in A.D. 70. His hearers asked Jesus when it would happen. They thought this would be the end of the world and the beginning of the eternal age.

Jesus warned them not to be deceived about the time of the end. They were to guard against people claiming falsely to be the Messiah (v.8). Also they were not to conclude hastily that every war was a sign of the end (v.9). In time would come international wars and catastrophes of various kinds (vv.10–11). Before the end Christians would be persecuted and tried in the highest courts for their faith. Jesus advised them to look on such trials as opportunities to testify for him (v.13). They were not to be afraid at this prospect. Jesus would help them have the words and wisdom to say the right thing (v.15). He advised them further that trouble and persecution might come from unexpected sources, even from relatives and friends (v.16). However, not a hair of their head would perish. This did not mean they wouldn't suffer but that no one could take them away from God.

Then Jesus began to answer the question that had been asked about when the destruction of the Temple would happen. He said it would happen in connection with the fall of Jerusalem (v.20). He advised people to flee Jerusalem at that time and he warned that Jerusalem would be destroyed and her citizens displaced.

Remember, no trouble comes that God did not foresee.

THE END OF TIME

Luke 21:25–38

How greatly should we be concerned about the end of time? This is a subject about which there is much uncertainty. Bible scholars do not agree about which passages refer to the end times. Furthermore, the meaning of the passages is not always clear. But the matter is important. One's view of the end of time determines how he will interpret historical events. For the Christian who believes that this age will climax with God's intervention in the person of Christ, history comes to be the working out of the divine plan.

After Jesus had spoken about the coming destruction of the Temple and Jerusalem, he talked about great phenomena in space and upon the earth (v.25). This would be a time of fear. Then the Son of man would come in a cloud with power and glory (v.27). The nearness of redemption would be an occasion for hope.

The hearers of Jesus were likely still wondering when these things would occur. Jesus said that, as the new leaves on a tree heralded summer, so the things he had spoken of would indicate the nearness of the kingdom of God (v.31). It is difficult to know what Jesus meant in saying that this generation would not pass away till all this had happened. Was he referring back now to the destruction of Jerusalem? Was he saying that mankind would not die out before God's plan was fulfilled? Even heaven and earth would disappear before Jesus' words would fail (v.33).

For us, as for his hearers, this warning means to be alert and not to be distracted by evil habits or worries. They were counseled to pray for strength to escape the coming hardships and to stand in the presence of the Son of man.

In these last days of Jesus he spent the nights in prayer on the Mount of Olives and the days in teaching in the Temple. What better example could we ask for?

A TOOL OF SATAN

Luke 22:1–6

The world has had its archtraitors. At the head of the list is Judas. How can such treachery as that of Judas be explained? What makes a potential friend become a fiend? From time to time we see a friendship, a business partnership, or a marriage break up as though one of the parties had become devil-possessed. Judas is the best-known example.

The time of the passover was near. The chief priests and the legal experts had already agreed to kill Jesus. Their problem was how to do it without inflaming the people (v.2). Jerusalem was filled with thousands and thousands of visitors for the passover. The custom at this season was to bring extra Roman soldiers from neighboring garrisons. The whole situation was explosive and Jesus had added to it by his triumphal entry and daily teaching in the Temple. His enemies were afraid to arrest him publicly for fear of an immediate uprising of the crowds in the city. Somehow, they had not learned that he was spending the nights on the Mount of Olives. Then came help they hadn't dared hope for.

One of the twelve defected. Many have tried to explain Judas' action. Was he a dissillusioned man? Was he an eager revolutionary who thought that the crowds would revolt to save Jesus? Was he trying to force Jesus into making a use of his divine power to establish his kingdom? Was he simply after the thirty silver pieces? Whatever else he was, he was a man who had permitted the devil to have access to his life. And, now, in the crucial time he became the devil's tool in bringing about the death of Christ. Satan entered into him (v.3). From there on the actions were the mechanics of evil —communication with the enemy, agreement on price, solemn promise, seeking the opportunity for the act (vv.4–6).

Resist Satan with all of your might or he may lead you into an act that would rival that of Judas.

THE PLACE FOR THE LAST MEAL

Luke 22:7–13

The question has been asked from time to time, "What would you do if you only had twenty four hours to live?" Note what Jesus did on his last night.

If a countdown had been going for the death of Jesus, the last critical twenty-four hours would have gotten under way. The day for the sacrifice of the passover lamb had come (v.7). It was time to begin to prepare for that night's supper of remembrance.

The assignment to get the place ready was given to Peter and John (v.8). Evidently the place had been prearranged by Jesus. Likely he had conferred with a disciple who lived in Jerusalem. Secrecy at this time was important. Jesus was safe from the attack of his enemies as long as he was surrounded by crowds. He had been spending the nights in seclusion on the Mount of Olives. Desiring to eat the passover in Jerusalem he must have agreed with a disciple living there on the use of an upper room in his house. He told Peter and John to go to the edge of the city where they would find a man carrying a pitcher (v.10). The man would be easy to locate because men did not carry pitchers since this was a woman's work. He gave them words to say so that they could identify themselves (v.11). The man would then take them to his home and show them a large furnished room on the second floor. If typical, this room was reached by an outside staircase. In it were cushions on the floor and a large low table. This would have been the normal furniture for such a dinner.

Peter and John found all as they had been instructed and proceeded to prepare the passover meal.

On his last night Jesus chose to eat with his followers and thereby to commemorate God's providential deliverance of his people from bondage.

Magnify your companionship with your Christian friends.

THE LORD'S SUPPER

Luke 22:14–23

Christians disagree about the meaning of the Lord's Supper but keep on observing it. Why has it endured? One needs to read the accounts of it in other Gospels as well as in 1 Corinthians 11:23–29.

On Jesus' last night he and the twelve gathered around the table. He had looked forward to this meal (v.15). He used the meal as a prophetic illustration of what the coming kingdom of God would be like (v.16).

Luke described Jesus taking the cup, praying, and telling his disciples to share it (v.16). Jesus was saying that all he had to leave them or to give them was that which he would accomplish by shedding his blood for them. In the other accounts of the Lord's Supper the bread was first and then the cup. Again Jesus referred to the coming kingdom of God (v.18). Of the bread he said, "This is my body" (v.19). This statement was not hard for the disciples to understand. He was present physically and so the bread was obviously to represent his body.

Some ancient manuscripts do not have verses 19*b*–20 and some do. Therefore, you will find some translators including them and some not. These words are like those in 1 Corinthians and were probably the words used by early Christians in this observance. The cup was called the new testament or the new covenant which leads us to compare Christ's deliverance of people to Moses' deliverance of the Israelites.

The Lord's Supper is a marvelous memorial appealing to all five of the senses thereby implanting its significance more firmly in the mind.

Jesus revealed during the evening that one of them would betray him and spoke ominously of the traitor's fate.

Let us be grateful for the reminder that we have in the Lord's Supper of what Christ has done for us.

LAST INSTRUCTIONS

Luke 22:24–38

Loved ones have cherished the last words of a dying person. Final instructions seem to be more important. Luke reported only a few of the words of Jesus on this last night in comparison to John's account.

The disciples of Jesus sensed that the climax was at hand. They argued about which of them would become leaders (v.24). Rather than being shocked at them Jesus showed great patience. He advised them that the greatest would be the one who served (v.26). This must have seemed paradoxical to them. However, most people have a hard time realizing how important it is to serve. Jesus then gave them a glimpse of the great blessings in store for them. He made them a double promise. They would share in his fellowship and they would share in his authority (v.30).

Jesus addressed Simon directly. He told him that Satan had wanted to sift all of them like wheat (v.31). This is somewhat like Satan challenging Job's devotion to God. Judas wasn't the only follower of Jesus whom the devil was seeking to influence. Jesus had prayed for his followers. He is our intercessor to plead our case. He implied to Peter that he would not be loyal. But after turning back to Christ, Peter was to strengthen the others as brothers (v.32). With impetuous force Peter insisted he would go to the limit for Christ (v.33). Jesus spoke specifically then of his denial.

Jesus asked his disciples if they remembered how well they had got along when they went on their tour without resources. They remembered (v.35). Jesus advised them they would be on their own now. If they were going to depend on a sword, they had better buy one (v.36). Their lives were in danger. They said they had two swords. Jesus said it was enough. They were really two too many.

Who needs a sword! The Word is our sword.

AGONY

Luke 22:39–46

Some may go through life without experiencing either ecstasy or agony. But Jesus knew both to the fullest. His agony was the greatest as he closed the last door of escape and started down the corridor of final commitment to the cross.

After his last meal with the disciples he took them out to the Mount of Olives where they had spent the last several nights (v.39). He urged them to pray in view of what was coming. Other Gospel accounts tell that he took three of the disciples with him a little distance and then he went on by himself about as far as you could throw a stone (v.41).

Jesus prayed and some of his words could be heard by the disciples. He had come to the last possible moment when he could turn back. The ordeal ahead of him had become clearer in his mind. No one knew better than Jesus what death meant. But there was to be more to his than physical suffering. As he had joined sinners in baptism at the Jordan, he was now to die the death of every sinner. It was the bitterest cup ever put to the lips of anyone. Jesus recoiled from it and asked for it to be removed if it would not thwart God's plan (v.42). Then he added, "Not my will, but thine, be done." This is the example for every follower of his.

The turning point had been reached and an angel from heaven came and strengthened him (v.43). Not all of the ancient manuscripts include the reference to the angel nor to the bloodlike sweat.

With full commitment to the course ahead of him and with renewed strength he came back to the disciples and found them sleeping (v.45). He aroused them, reminding them he had told them to pray in view of what was coming.

Whatever you are facing, you can find help by remembering how Jesus prepared for the horrible experience that was ahead of him. You can pray, "Thy will be done."

ARRESTED

Luke 22:47–53

What would you do if trapped with no escape? Jesus acted as if he were in charge when he was surrounded and arrested.

The lights and sounds of the arresting party in the distance may have caused Jesus to come from his lonely prayer vigil to arouse his disciples. As he awakened them, a crowd burst into the garden. Judas led them (v.47). He rushed to Jesus and kissed him. A modest kiss was an appropriate greeting from a disciple to his master but Judas made a show of it. Jesus asked him if he had agreed to identify him in this manner (v.48).

The followers of Jesus impulsively thought of resistance and called to him for directions (v.49). Not waiting for the answer one of them swung his sword at a man's head. He would have got him but the man dodged and lost only his ear (v.50). Jesus halted the violence and healed the man's ear. If Jesus had wanted help, he could have called all of the forces of heaven.

He spoke to the leaders of the arresting party. They included the highest officers of the Temple and of the people. He reprimanded them for coming against him as though he were an insurrectionist (v.52). Evidently his greatest concern was for his disciples. He was anxious that they not be molested and be permitted to go free at this time. The authorities needed to understand that his people were not political revolutionaries. He reminded his enemies that at no time had he hidden from them or sought to avoid arrest (v.53). Jesus told his opponents that he recognized this hour was theirs and that it was a dark and evil hour. Satan has never exercised greater power than he did that night and the day following. Jesus' words pointed to the limit of this effort.

Be assured that Christ will take care of his own in the darkest hour.

THE BREAKING POINT

Luke 22:54–62

Everyone lives under pressure. How much could you stand? Don't be too sure of yourself! Remember Simon Peter. He said he would be willing to go to prison or even to die for Jesus.

Peter had as much courage or more than any of the other disciples. He followed Jesus even to the high priest's house and gained entrance. He joined a group gathered around a fire in the courtyard (v.55). It may have been his nervous movements in trying to catch a glimpse of Jesus that caught the attention of a maidservant. She came up to him, studied his face intently, and identified him as having been with Jesus (v.56). He tried to brush her off by saying that he didn't know the man. He had broken. He had lied and didn't even realize it yet. Later someone else accused him to his face of being a disciple and he said that he wasn't (v.58). An hour passed and someone recognizing his Galilean dialect charged him with being an associate of Jesus. Peter made his strongest denial. As he did, he heard a cock crowing. He looked toward the house. Jesus was standing at a window or balcony and he looked at Peter (v.61). Peter came to himself. When he saw Jesus, he broke further. He remembered how the Lord had warned him he would deny him. This couldn't be happening to him. He had ruined himself as a follower of Christ. His hope for Christ's intervention in the affairs of men had failed. Now he had lied and lost his self-respect. He was crushed. His action reported here is that with which many can identify—into the night to weep tears of repentance. Surely Peter remembered that Jesus had said to him, "When you turn back, strengthen your brethren."

Every person who has strayed needs to think through this experience of Peter. Turn back to Christ, find new strength and use it to help others.

THE CHARGE

Luke 22:63–71

People always try to make their actions seem reasonable. No one wants to admit he acts irrationally or insanely. Some of the most terrible acts have been committed by people who were convinced they were acting reasonably.

Jesus was in the hands of people who had laid aside reason and conscience. A madness had possessed them. The men guarding him invented a savage and merciless game. They blindfolded him and struck him in the face knocking him down. Then they would challenge him as he lay on the floor to identify who hit him (vv.63–64). Furthermore, they subjected him to the abuse of barrack room profanity (v.65).

With daylight the Sanhedrin could lawfully assemble and Christ was brought in for a hearing (v.66). The purpose of the assembly was to formulate a charge. They asked him directly if he was the Christ and he refused to answer them. Jesus had not positively affirmed that he was the expected Messiah. The reason he avoided this was probably because of the concept that people had in general about the Messiah. Their hopes were high that the Messiah would be a political military leader. Jesus had definitely used messianic terms and had performed specific messianic actions. Why didn't he correct his questioners? He told them that if he asked them anything, they wouldn't answer him. Then he boldly proclaimed himself to be the Son of man who would sit at the right hand of God (v.69). It was clear to the Sanhedrin what he meant but they wanted to charge him with blasphemy to discredit him with the people. And so they asked him if he was the Son of God. He indicated that this was their choice of terms and they took this response to be grounds for charging him with blasphemy.

Let us affirm courageously that Jesus is the Christ, the Son of God.

116

UNIT
11

Death: Horror and Grandeur

Every man's tragedy is death. No one escapes it. It is like a cruel competitor who always wins. Life may be compared to a desperate game in which we always lose. The winner stepping forward to claim the victory is death. But death has lost its sting and the grave its victory (1 Cor. 15:55). A new champion has overthrown death and offers life to all who will join him. The contest was the struggle described in chapters 23 and 24 of Luke.

Christ Jesus died the death of every man. He replaced Adam as the head of the human race. In Adam we all die but in Christ we are made alive. His death came upon his condemnation in the courts of men. The issue was clarified in the Jewish court and then it was purposefully clouded from there on. The issue was his messiahship and his divinity. Jesus was either Christ, the Messiah, Son of God, or an imposter. The examination was not to determine the validity of his claim but only to discover if he had made such a claim. Becoming convinced that he had offered himself as the Messiah the Jewish authorities did not seek to decide his legitimacy. They simply rejected him and conspired for his death.

Jesus experienced death as it was inflicted upon the vilest of men. Dying is a lonely action and yet every man experiences it. However, with Christ's death it need not be a lonely experience for anyone else. Every person committing himself to Christ may be assured of the Lord's presence even as he traverses the corridor of death. Jesus did more than die on the cross. He atoned for the sins of mankind. This turns life into a "new ball game." The determining element of life now is one's relation to Christ.

If death is all, then despair is the logical emotion for the human race. What can anything amount to? What difference do brief moments of pleasure make? If Christ had stayed in the grave, the best place for human beings would have been hiding from one another. But death is not the end of life. Christ proved this.

Hope is not just wishing in the face of the impossible. It must have some ground on which to stand. It began to rise with the disciples when the tomb was discovered to be empty. But an empty tomb wasn't enough to turn terrified men into bold champions willing to die for their Lord. Jesus Christ appeared to his followers after his resurrection. He walked with them. He instructed them. He commissioned them with the responsibility to win the world to him. This would call for total commitment on their part plus divine power.

Every age has made its unique response to the gospel of Christ. Perhaps, never yet have gains been made that would be comparable to those in the lifetime of the first followers of Christ. But our day is yet to be measured. What will Christians of the space age church do for Christ? Can we utilize the marvelous instruments and techniques at hand to acquaint millions with Jesus Christ? Let us, wherever we are and using whatever means are available, bring men to follow Christ and teach them all that he has commanded.

ON TRIAL

Luke 23:1–12

The courtroom is the setting for many modern dramas. Even a spectator can get excited watching a person on trial. Jesus was put on trial not only before the Sanhedrin but also before both Pilate and then Herod.

The members of the Sanhedrin brought Jesus to Pilate because they were not allowed by Rome to pronounce the death sentence. They had decided as far as their own laws were concerned that Jesus was guilty of blasphemy by saying falsely that he was the Son of God. They couldn't use this as a charge in a Roman court and so they prepared another charge against him to Pilate. They said that he was undermining the people's allegiance to Rome, that he was advising them to withhold paying taxes, and that he was campaigning for the position of king (v.2). Pilate probably saw through their charges, but they were serious enough that he had to investigate them. He questioned Jesus directly about being King of the Jews. Jesus had never used terminology like this and told Pilate so (v.3). Pilate saw that Jesus was not a wild revolutionary and pronounced him innocent. An uproar came from the Sanhedrin members as they tried to impress Pilate that Jesus had made trouble from Galilee to Jerusalem. The governor immediately sent Jesus to Herod Antipas, ruler of Galilee, who was visiting in the city at the Passover time (v.7).

Herod was delighted to have Jesus in his hands. Now he could see what he was like. He tried to get him to work a miracle (v.8). Jesus had absolutely no word for Herod even when questioned. To Herod, Jesus was nothing but a joke. He led his troops in laughing at him and humiliating him as the Temple guards had done (v.11). Then he sent him back to Pilate and the two rulers were friends thereafter.

No one can pass to someone else the decision he must make about Christ.

CONDEMNED TO DIE

Luke 23:13–25

What if you had someone's life in your hands and you could save it? But, if in saving it you would be ruined, what would you do? That was Pilate's situation.

When Jesus was sent back to him, Pilate called the officials and people together and for a second time pronounced Jesus innocent of the charges made against him (v.14). Luke's report of the agreement of Pilate and Herod on the innocence of Jesus is a significant record for all ages to come. Pilate offered to have Jesus flogged and turn him loose. The releasing of a prisoner was appropriate at the Passover. The crowd began to cry for the release of Barabbas. This man was actually guilty of the crimes Jesus had been falsely accused of (v.19). This proved that the Jewish leaders were not sincere in their charges. Pilate got the attention of the crowd and tried again to get them to support his decision to release Jesus.

The crowd had found a leader who could be intimidated. They cried out for Jesus to be crucified. Pilate asked why and again said he would scourge Jesus and let him go. The demand for crucifixion became a roaring chant (v.23).

Pilate's career was at stake. He had confronted the Jewish leaders before and had been made to back down. They knew he would yield to them again. He feared the possibility of a complaint about him being sent to Rome. And so, finally he nodded and delivered the sentence that was being demanded by the crowd (v.24). He released to them a man who was recognized as an enemy of Rome. From the standpoint of Roman justice Barabbas should have been executed on the cross that was used for Jesus. He went free and Jesus was turned over to the executioners.

Do we use all the opportunities we have to witness courageously for Jesus? It isn't easy to do, is it?

THE EXECUTION OF JESUS

Luke 23:26–38

The horribleness of death is intensified if it is an execution. To be executed is to suffer a death not meant for a human being. The executed is judged not to be qualified for human society and unfit to live.

Beaten by the Temple guards and again by Herod's soldiers and then flogged by the Romans, Jesus was too weak to carry his cross. Simon of Cyrene in Africa, possibly a Passover visitor, was drafted to carry Jesus' cross (v.26). Some think from Mark 15:21 that this man and his two sons became Christians.

Women were following the group weeping. Jesus told them not to weep for him but for Jerusalem in view of a worse fate coming to it. If the Romans would do this to him in times that were pleasant like spring, what would they do when revolution would become like a season of drought (v.31)? Three crosses stood on a hill that day but in time Romans filled the area with rebelling Jews hanging on crosses.

Some manuscripts do not have the record of Jesus praying for forgiveness of his executioners (v.34) but some scholars argue strongly for its validity. It is typical of Jesus.

The scene around the crucifixion was repulsive. People stood and stared in horror at Jesus dying. The leaders of the people mocked him and called on him to prove his messiahship by saving himself (v.35). The Roman soldiers entered into the spirit of the profane humor and told him to save himself and prove he was King of the Jews. Over his head was a placard designating him as King of the Jews (v.38) which was Pilate's feeble effort to strike back at the Jewish officials. He had ordered this placard because a criminal being executed was supposed to have the charge against him displayed.

When it seems hard to be a Christian, remember the price Christ paid for you to have the privilege.

THE PROMISE OF PARADISE

Luke 23:39–43

What if at your death Jesus would appear to you and promise to take you to be with him forever! This promise was made to one of the thieves dying at the side of Jesus.

One of the criminals hanging near Jesus joined those mocking and taunting him (v.39). This action accentuated the impropriety of the scene. Here were those who were supposed to be God's chosen people killing the very Son of God. Joining them in reviling Jesus was a criminal who deserved the death he was getting but who knew in his heart that Jesus was innocent. The other thief reprimanded this one and admonished him to think how improper his words were (vv.40–41).

Then the penitent thief addressed Jesus. His words must have been heard gladly by Christ. It had been a long, painful experience from the time of his midnight prayer about ten or twelve hours before this. He had suffered almost every humiliation that could be heaped upon him. But here as he was dying a stranger voiced faith in him. The faith was evidently accompanied by ignorance and preceded by a life of sin but a man who had nothing in this world to gain asked Jesus to remember him. One of the brightest promises Jesus ever made was spoken to this man. Christ told him that on that day he would become his companion in paradise (v.43). What a way to die! In the presence of Jesus, seeing his smile, hearing his voice, and being assured of his eternal presence! On the other hand, how comforting it is to us to know that, as Jesus died, he heard again an expression of faith in him. None of his disciples were able to follow him through the death experience but he gained a disciple on the cross to accompany him into paradise.

The question has been asked, "Where is this paradise?" and the answer has been given that it is where Jesus is.

DEAD AND BURIED

Luke 23:44–56

In a situation where a person is suffering extremely, death is considered a blessing. Crucifixion was one of the cruellest and most painful executions devised by man. Men had been known to survive a full week and to become raving mad in their pain and suffering. Jesus' death was no doubt hastened by his night of agony, his two beatings, and the flogging.

At the sixth hour or noon darkness came upon Jerusalem and the area around. This was not an eclipse for an eclipse is impossible at the time of a full moon. The date of the Passover was changed annually so it would come during the full moon. In addition to this the veil of the Temple was torn perhaps by an earthquake (v.45). This has been looked on as a sign that access to God is open to everyone in Christ.

Jesus gave a great cry. This may have been a shout of victory. Then he prayed a prayer Jewish children were taught as a bedtime prayer (Ps. 31:5) but he added the word "Father" (v.46). And he died.

Reactions varied. The Roman centurion voiced his opinion of Jesus' innocence (v.47). People slapped their chests in distress (v.48). Disciples of Jesus stood afar off watching (v.49).

A prominent member of the Sanhedrin by the name of Joseph of Arimathea was concerned. He had not voted for the death of Jesus. As was proper he went to Pilate and requested the body of Jesus (v.52). He must have acted in sorrow and tenderness in handling the body. He removed it from the cross, wrapped it in clean linen, and laid it in a tomb carved back into a stone hillside where no one had yet been laid (v.53). The women accompanied him to note the location. The next day was the sabbath but they would come early the day after which was the first day of the week.

What do you think now about Jesus? Will you serve him?

CHRIST IS NOT DEAD

Luke 24:1–12

Some things are said to be too good to be true. The resurrection of Christ is one of those events that could be so described. Luke reported it with reservation. He didn't seek to set forth a comprehensive account but rather the specific incidents that would help his readers believe in the resurrection and understand it.

When the sabbath was over at sundown, the women who had followed Jesus probably began preparing spices to insert into the wrappings of the body of Jesus. With the dawning light they went to the tomb (v.1). The stone that had covered the entrance was rolled to one side. Stepping in they looked but could not find a body (v.3). This disturbed and confused them. What had happened? Suddenly standing right next to them were two men whose very clothes were radiant. Luke did not identify these two heavenly messengers for us. Instead he concentrated on reporting their message. They advised the women not to look for the living among the dead. Christ had risen (v.6). They reminded them how he had prophesied regarding his own death and resurrection (v.7). The women agreed that they did remember.

They hurried back to tell the disciples who had evidently been staying together since the crucifixion (v.9). For the record Luke identified who these women were which might mean that in his gathering of information from eyewitnesses he had talked to them (v.10). The women's report, though, was incredible to the disciples. Believing in the resurrection of Christ and accepting his lordship is not easy to do. It is an act of faith. Peter and John verified the report by going to the tomb. Some old manuscripts do not include verse 12 but it has essentially the same information as that in John 20:3–6.

Christ has risen. Believe it and rejoice.

A WALK WITH CHRIST

Luke 24:13–35

A person must be ready to learn some things before he can learn them. Learning readiness may come from meeting a problem, discussing what is involved, and seeking a solution.

Two who might be called lesser disciples left Jerusalem to walk to Emmaus a few miles away (v.13). They were deep in conversation and hardly realized that someone was catching up with them. This was Jesus but somehow they did not recognize him. It may have been because they were walking into the evening sun, because of his appearance either from the beatings and crucifixion or the transformation in the resurrection, because they didn't expect to see him, or because they were miraculously hindered. When asked what they were talking about, they reviewed their hopes, their disappointment, and their present confusion (vv.19–24).

Then Jesus spoke to them and helped them understand what had happened. He told them that suffering preceded glory (v.26). Then he taught them as they walked. Quotations were used from Moses, from the prophets, and from all portions of the Scriptures (v.27).

They had come to Emmaus and it was evening. They stopped but Jesus walked on. They called to him and he consented to stay with them (v.29). It was as they ate that they recognized him. When he broke bread and passed it to them, they knew him (vv.30–31). It is in close fellowship with Jesus that we know him. He vanished but they were aglow from the experience (v.32). It was night by now but they hurried back to Jerusalem. They were met with the positive assertion from the others that they also knew Christ had risen because he had appeared to Simon (v.34).

A walk with Christ will warm your heart and open your eyes.

GRADUATION AND COMMENCEMENT

Luke 24:36–53

Students who persevere are graduated from their studies and urged to commence using what they have learned in life. Jesus' resurrection appearances were like a graduation and commencement experience for his followers. A training phase was ended and the disciples were sent out to witness.

Jesus appeared to the eleven as they heard the report from the two who had walked with him on the Emmaus road (v.36). They were frightened at first and thought they were seeing a ghost. Some people still have a hard time realizing Jesus was as human as he appeared to be.

Jesus reassured them. He called attention to his hands and feet and invited them to touch him (v.39). They still doubted their senses. Jesus asked for something to eat and ate in their presence. This seemed to convince them. To help them further he reminded that he had told them in advance what would happen (v.44). Then he substantiated what he was saying with Scripture references (v.45).

As Jesus helped his disciples to understand the resurrection, he began to reconfirm in their minds their responsibility to proclaim the good news. He was calling upon them to undertake a worldwide ministry of preaching in his name (v.47). They had heard him and seen him and they were to be his witnesses everywhere. They would need power for this task and it would come from God. They were to wait in Jerusalem until they received it (v.49). In this way they were prepared for the coming of the Holy Spirit at Pentecost.

The resurrection appearances lasted for a few weeks and then ceased with the ascension. With this the disciples became radiant and effective witnesses (v.52).

This completes our study of Luke. Congratulations on your perseverance. Can you put to use what you have learned? Let your days be filled with praise and witnessing for Christ.

For Further Study

ALLEN, CLIFTON J. *The Broadman Bible Commentary,* Vol. 9. Nashville: Broadman Press, 1969.

CARGILL, ROBERT L. *All the Parables of Jesus.* Nashville: Broadman Press, 1970.

ROBERTSON, A. T. *Word Pictures in the New Testament,* Vol. 2. Nashville: Broadman Press, 1943.

TURLINGTON, HENRY E. *Luke's Witness to Jesus.* Nashville: Broadman Press, 1967.